Hands-On Computer Vision with Julia

Build complex applications with advanced Julia packages for image processing, neural networks, and Artificial Intelligence

Dmitrijs Cudihins

BIRMINGHAM - MUMBAI

Hands-On Computer Vision with Julia

Commissioning Editor: Aaron Lazar
Acquisition Editor: Sandeep Mishra
Content Development Editor: Tiksha Sarang
Technical Editor: Supriya Thabe
Copy Editors: Safis Editing, Vikrant Phadkay
Project Coordinator: Prajakta Naik
Proofreader: Safis Editing
Indexer: Aiswarya Narayanan
Graphics: Jisha Chirayil
Production Coordinator: Arvindkumar Gupta

First published: June 2018

Production reference: 1290618

Published by Packt Publishing Ltd.
Livery Place
35 Livery Street
Birmingham
B3 2PB, UK.

ISBN 978-1-78899-879-6

www.packtpub.com

`mapt.io`

Mapt is an online digital library that gives you full access to over 5,000 books and videos, as well as industry leading tools to help you plan your personal development and advance your career. For more information, please visit our website.

Why subscribe?

- Spend less time learning and more time coding with practical eBooks and Videos from over 4,000 industry professionals

- Improve your learning with Skill Plans built especially for you

- Get a free eBook or video every month

- Mapt is fully searchable

- Copy and paste, print, and bookmark content

PacktPub.com

Did you know that Packt offers eBook versions of every book published, with PDF and ePub files available? You can upgrade to the eBook version at `www.PacktPub.com` and, as a print book customer, you are entitled to a discount on the eBook copy. Get in touch with us at `service@packtpub.com` for more details.

At `www.PacktPub.com`, you can also read a collection of free technical articles, sign up for a range of free newsletters, and receive exclusive discounts and offers on Packt books and eBooks.

Contributors

About the author

Dmitrijs Cudihins is a skilled data scientist, machine learning engineer, and software developer with more than eight years' commercial experience. His started off as a web developer, but later switched to data science and computer vision. He has been a senior data scientist for the last three years, providing consultancy services for a state-owned enterprise. There, he uses Julia to automate communication with citizens, applying different CV techniques and scanned image processing.

About the reviewer

Zhuo Qingliang (KDr2 online) works for *paodingai*, a fintech start-up in China that is dedicated to improving the financial industry using AI technologies. He has over 10 years' experience in Linux, C, C++, Java, Python, and Perl development. He is interested in programming, consulting, and participating in, and contributing to, the open source community (which naturally includes the Julia community). He maintains a website, *KDr2*, where you can find out more about him.

Packt is searching for authors like you

If you're interested in becoming an author for Packt, please visit authors.packtpub.com and apply today. We have worked with thousands of developers and tech professionals, just like you, to help them share their insight with the global tech community. You can make a general application, apply for a specific hot topic that we are recruiting an author for, or submit your own idea.

Table of Contents

Preface

Through this book, there will be a thorough guidance for all developers who want to get started with building computer vision applications using Julia. Julia is well suited for image processing because of its ease of use and the fact that it lets you write easy-to-compile and efficient machine code.

Readers will be taken through various packages that support image processing in Julia, and will also tap into open source libraries such as Open CV and Tesseract to find optimum solutions to problems encountered in computer vision. They will learn to build a full-fledged image processing application using JuliaImages, perform basic to advanced image and video stream processing with Julia's APIs, and much more.

Who this book is for

This book is for all those Julia developers who are interested in learning how to perform image processing, for those who want to explore the field of computer vision and wish to benefit from this book. A basic knowledge of Julia will help you understand concepts more effectively.

What this book covers

Chapter 1, *Getting Started with JuliaImages*, is about getting your first introduction to JuliaImages and ImageCore packages. We will be loading images from various sources and creating thumbnails, that is resizing and saving them back on disk in a different file format.

Chapter 2, *Image Enhancement*, is all about working with the ImageFiltering package. We will understand what linear and nonlinear filtering operations are and how they can be used to transform images, such as sharpening, blurring, and smoothing.

Chapter 3, *Image Adjustment*, will guide you through the ImageMorphology package. Morphological transformations are some simple operations based on the image shape that allow you to remove small noise, shrink objects, separate objects, and increase the object size or background space.

Chapter 4, *Image Segmentation*, will explore the ImageSegmentation package. Readers will learn how to use supervised and unsupervised methods to simplify or represent an image into something that is more meaningful and easier to analyze.

Chapter 5, *Image Representation*, will explore the ImageFeatures package. We will learn to compute compact descriptors or "features" in a form that permits comparison and matching of two images.

Chapter 6, *Introduction to Neural Networks*, will demonstrate the need for neural networks. We'll cover getting, preparing the data, and improving and predicting the images. This chapter will also teach you to classify datasets, training and putting it all together.

Chapter 7, *Using Pre-Trained Neural Networks*, will introduce you to pre-trained networks and help in predicting image classes using Inception V3 and MobileNet V2. It will also help to extract features generated by Inception V3 and MobileNet V2 and cover transfer learning using Inception V3.

Chapter 8, *OpenCV*, will demonstrate how to use the open source Open CV library to perform real-time computer vision analysis. We will learn to find faces on images and then track them on a video stream.

Chapter 9, *Case Study – Book Cover Classification, Analysis and Recognition*, will incorporate the various techniques that we've described all along the book to develop a Book cover classification, analysis, and recognition project.

To get the most out of this book

1. We are required to have Julia v. 1.0 or above installed
2. We need to ensure that our Julia environment has all the required prerequisites mentioned in every chapter

Download the example code files

You can download the example code files for this book from your account at www.packtpub.com. If you purchased this book elsewhere, you can visit www.packtpub.com/support and register to have the files emailed directly to you.

You can download the code files by following these steps:

1. Log in or register at www.packtpub.com.
2. Select the **SUPPORT** tab.
3. Click on **Code Downloads & Errata**.
4. Enter the name of the book in the **Search** box and follow the onscreen instructions.

Once the file is downloaded, please make sure that you unzip or extract the folder using the latest version of:

- WinRAR/7-Zip for Windows
- Zipeg/iZip/UnRarX for Mac
- 7-Zip/PeaZip for Linux

The code bundle for the book is also hosted on GitHub at `https://github.com/PacktPublishing/Hands-On-Computer-Vision-with-Julia`. In case there's an update to the code, it will be updated on the existing GitHub repository.

We also have other code bundles from our rich catalog of books and videos available at `https://github.com/PacktPublishing/`. Check them out!

Download the color images

We also provide a PDF file that has color images of the screenshots/diagrams used in this book. You can download it here: `https://www.packtpub.com/sites/default/files/downloads/HandsOnComputerVisionwithJulia_ColorImages.pdf`.

Conventions used

There are a number of text conventions used throughout this book.

`CodeInText`: Indicates code words in text, database table names, folder names, filenames, file extensions, pathnames, dummy URLs, user input, and Twitter handles. Here is an example: "You can confirm your version number by typing `VERSION` in the Julia console or REPL."

A block of code is set as follows:

```
using Images

sample_image_path = "sample-images/cats-3061372_640.jpg";
sample_image = nothing

if isfile(sample_image_path)
    sample_image = load(sample_image_path);
else
    info("ERROR: Image not found!")
end
```

When we wish to draw your attention to a particular part of a code block, the relevant lines or items are set in bold:

```
using Images, ImageView
  img = load("sample-images/cats-3061372_640.jpg");
  imshow(img);
```

Any command-line input or output is written as follows:

```
julia> using Images
julia> pwd()
"/Users/dc/reps/packt-julia"
```

 Warnings or important notes appear like this.

 Tips and tricks appear like this.

Get in touch

Feedback from our readers is always welcome.

General feedback: Email feedback@packtpub.com and mention the book title in the subject of your message. If you have questions about any aspect of this book, please email us at questions@packtpub.com.

Errata: Although we have taken every care to ensure the accuracy of our content, mistakes do happen. If you have found a mistake in this book, we would be grateful if you would report this to us. Please visit www.packtpub.com/submit-errata, selecting your book, clicking on the Errata Submission Form link, and entering the details.

Piracy: If you come across any illegal copies of our works in any form on the Internet, we would be grateful if you would provide us with the location address or website name. Please contact us at copyright@packtpub.com with a link to the material.

If you are interested in becoming an author: If there is a topic that you have expertise in and you are interested in either writing or contributing to a book, please visit authors.packtpub.com.

Reviews

Please leave a review. Once you have read and used this book, why not leave a review on the site that you purchased it from? Potential readers can then see and use your unbiased opinion to make purchase decisions, we at Packt can understand what you think about our products, and our authors can see your feedback on their book. Thank you!

For more information about Packt, please visit `packtpub.com`.

1
Getting Started with JuliaImages

This chapter is all about introducing the `JuliaImages` collection. `JuliaImages` is a collection of different packages that are used for image processing. We will look into the `Images.jl` and `ImagesMetadata.jl` packages, load and preview images from various sources, read metadata, resize and scale images, create thumbnails, and save them back to disk in a different format.

In this chapter, we will cover the following topics:

- Setting up Julia
- Reading images from various sources
- Saving images in different formats
- Cropping, scaling, and resizing images
- Rotating images
- Using test images

Technical requirements

Users are required to have Julia v. 1.0 or above installed. Julia can be downloaded from the official page at `https://julialang.org/downloads/`.

You can confirm your version number by typing `VERSION` into the Julia console or REPL, as shown in the following code snippet:

```
julia> VERSION
v"0.7.0-DEV.4465"
```

The Julia community does not keep sources other than the Julia website or GitHub up-to-date. Therefore, it is strongly advised to refer to the official website for the latest available version. For example, Ubuntu users get an older version when installing Julia using `apt-get`.

You should also clone or download a GitHub repository containing source code and sample images:

`https://github.com/PacktPublishing/Hands-On-Computer-Vision-with-Julia`

This can be done by going to the GitHub page and pressing either the **Clone or Download** button in the top right corner.

Setting up your Julia

Before we start working with our images, we need to ensure that our Julia environment has all the required prerequisites so that we can complete the chapter. We already confirmed that our Julia setup is correct, so let's proceed with installing the most essential packages from the `JuliaImages` collection.

Installing packages

The most essential packages from the `JuliaImages` collection are the following:

- `Images.jl`
- `ImageMetadata.jl`
- `ImageView.jl`
- `TestImages.jl`

These packages are all you need to perform simple tasks, and most regular users should be fine with the setup.

Run the following commands in the Julia REPL to get them installed and configured. If you have not used Julia before, it is very likely that these commands will install additional dependencies:

```
using Pkg
Pkg.add("Images")
Pkg.add("ImageMetadata")
Pkg.add("ImageView")
Pkg.add("TestImages")
Pkg.update()
```

The moment installation completes, it is advised that you verify whether the packages can be loaded. This is done by merely importing them into the current environment, waiting for new packages to compile, and seeing whether the command succeeds:

```
julia> using Images, ImageMetadata, TestImages, ImageView
```

There is a small chance that the preceding command will fail with an exception message stating that one of the packages does not exist:

```
ERROR: ArgumentError: Module XXX not found in current path.
Run `Pkg.add("XXX")` to install the TestImages package.
```

Please follow the instructions to install a missing package and repeat the steps from this chapter.

 Windows users are required to complete additional steps to make the TestImages package work. Users are required to follow an extensive post-installation guide from the package page, http://juliaimages. github.io/TestImages.jl/, or from Chapter 9, *Case Study – Book Cover Classification, Analysis, and Recognition.*

Reading images

There are multiple different sources for your images. Let's look into three of the most popular methods:

- Reading images from disk
- Reading images from URL
- Reading multiple images in a folder

Start by loading the `Images` package and verifying your current working directory using `pwd`:

```
julia> using Images
julia> pwd()
"/Users/dc/reps/packt-julia"
```

If `pwd` does not correspond to your project folder, you have two options:

- Start Julia from a folder that does correspond
- Use the `cd` function to change it

The `cd` function accepts a single argument—the local path. An example of using the `cd` function would be as follows:

```
cd("~/repositories/julia-hands-on") # Unix-like systems
cd("C:\\repositories\\julia-hands-on") # Windows users
```

When you are all set, you can proceed to load your first image.

Reading a single image from disk

Reading an image from disk is simple and is done by calling the `load` function.
The `load` function accepts a single argument—the image path—and returns an image object. The following code assigns an image to a custom variable.

We will be using the `sample-images` folder from the GitHub repository. You are required to have a functioning project folder when running the following code:

```
using Images

sample_image_path = "sample-images/cats-3061372_640.jpg";
sample_image = nothing

if isfile(sample_image_path)
    sample_image = load(sample_image_path);
else
    info("ERROR: Image not found!")
end
```

A typical problem users face is using the wrong path. The preceding code example implements a check to see whether the file exists and prints an error if it does not.

Reading a single image from a URL

The process of reading an image from a URL is first getting it downloaded to disk using the `download` function and then processing it, as in the preceding section:

```
image_url =
"https://cdn.pixabay.com/photo/2018/01/04/18/58/cats-3061372_640.jpg?attach
ment"
downloaded_image_path = download(image_url)
downloaded_image = load(downloaded_image_path)
```

Depending on your project, it might make sense to download the file to a custom folder. You can define a download location by sending it as a second parameter to the `download` function:

```
image_url =
"https://cdn.pixabay.com/photo/2018/01/04/18/58/cats-3061372_640.jpg?attach
ment"
downloaded_image_path = download(image_url, 'custom_image_name.jpg')
downloaded_image = load(downloaded_image_path)
```

 Copyright notice: Pixabay provides images under CC0 Creative Commons. They are free for commercial use and no attributions are required.

Reading images in a folder

Loading files from a directory is a common use case. This is done by identifying a list of files in a directory, filtering the necessary files, and then executing a set of operations for each and every one of them.

We will be using the `sample-images` folder from the GitHub repository. You are required to have a functioning project folder when running the following example:

```
using Images

directory_path = "sample-images";
directory_files = readdir(directory_path);
directory_images = filter(x -> ismatch(r"\.(jpg|png|gif){1}$"i, x),
directory_files);

for image_name in directory_images
  image_path = joinpath(directory_path, image_name);
```

```
    image = load(image_path);
    # other operations
end
```

This example introduces a number of new functions and techniques, which are explained as follows:

- We use `readdir` from the Julia Base to read all the files names in a directory
- We use `filter` from the Julia Base, as well as custom regular expressions to find files ending with `.jpg`, `.png`, or `.gif`, both in lower and upper-case
- We use the `for` loop to iterate over filtered names
- We use `joinpath` from the Julia Base to combine the directory name and filename so that we have a full path to the image
- We use the `load` function (which you have already learned about) to load the image

Please be aware that `readdir` returns filenames. This is the reason for us using `joinpath`, which joins components into a full path.

Saving images

You have already learned how to *load* and *download* images, so now it's time to learn how to save your image. We will use the `save` function from the `Images` package to save the image to disk.

The `save` function accepts two arguments:

- The destination file location and name
- The image object

Let's have a look at the code to save images:

```
# load an image
img = load("sample-images/cats-3061372_640.jpg")

# save file in JPG format
save("my_new_file.jpg", img)

# save file in PNG format
save("my_new_file.png", img)
```

The image format is chosen based on the filename extension. Please note that saving the image in different formats can affect the output quality and file size. Users should find a balance between size and quality.

The `save` function does not allow you to set *image quality*, which is usually available in graphics editors, such as GIMP.

Using test images

The `TestImages.jl` package and dataset provides easy access to a small number of free images out of the box. It is the way to go when trying out different computer vision techniques and algorithms.

The benefits of using the `TestImages` dataset are the following:

- Images are of different file types, such as JPG, PNG, and TIF
- Images are of different sizes, such as 512x512 and 256x256
- Images are of different color schemes, such as RGB and grayscale

It is very easy to start with the `TestImages` package. You just need to load the `TestImages` package and use the `testimage` function to load the image by name:

```
using TestImages
img = testimage("mandril_color");
save("mandril_color.png", img);
```

Our code example would result in loading a mandrill image from the `TestImages` dataset. You can save this in your current working directory.

Previewing images

You have already learned to load, download, and save images. The only way to check the image itself would be to go to the project folder and open it from there.

The `ImageView` package solves this problem by previewing the image directly from Julia:

```
using Images, ImageView
img = load("sample-images/cats-3061372_640.jpg");
imshow(img);
```

This will preview the image in a new window.

Cropping, scaling, and resizing

Now that you know how to load and preview your image, it is time to start working on content. Three of the most frequent activities you will do when working with images are as follows:

- **Crop**: Select a specific area of an image
- **Resize**: Change the size of an image without keeping the proportions
- **Scale**: Enlarge or shrink an image while keeping the proportions

Cropping an image

Let's go back to the image with the two cats we previewed recently. Here, we will create a new picture, which will only contain the cat on the right:

Our first step will be to identify an area of interest. We will do this by loading the image to Julia and checking its width and height:

```
using Images, ImageView
source_image = load("sample-images/cats-3061372_640.jpg");
size(source_image)
```

The `size` function will output (360, 640), which stands for 360px in height (*y*-axis) and 640px in width (*x*-axis). Both coordinates start from the top-left corner.

I have run a number of experiments and identified an area we are interested in—the height from 100 to 290 and the width from 280 to 540. You can try playing around with the following code to see how changing the region will affect the output:

```
cropped_image = img[100:290, 280:540];
imshow(cropped_image)
```

This will result in the following image being created and stored in the `cropped_image` variable. This will also allocate memory so that you can store the newly created image:

 Images are *vertical-major*, which means that this first index corresponds to the vertical axis and the second to the horizontal axis. This might be different from other programming languages.

There is also another way to create a cropped image, which is by creating a *view* to the original image. Views don't create a new object or allocate memory, they just point to the original image (or array). They are great when you want to analyze or change a specific part of the picture without interfering with the rest of it:

```
cropped_image_view = view(img, 100:290, 280:540);
imshow(cropped_image_view)
```

If you run the preceding code, you will see that it returns an identical result. You can also *save* the image to disk without any problems.

Resizing an image

Image resizing is the process of changing an image's size without keeping proportions. This is done by calling the `imresize` function and supplying a new width and height.

Let's take our image with the cats as an example and resize it to `100 x 250` so that we can see what has changed:

We will use our classic code and load the image from disk:

```
using Images, ImageView
source_image = load("sample-images/cats-3061372_640.jpg");
resized_image = imresize(source_image, (100, 250));
imshow(resized_image);
```

You should be able to see an image of a smaller size. It has a width of `250` pixels and a height of `100` pixels:

A typical example would be to resize an image to fit a square. You would need to pass the width and height as equal values:

```
using Images, ImageView
source_image = load("sample-images/cats-3061372_640.jpg");
resized_image = imresize(source_image, (200, 200));
imshow(resized_image);
```

This would result in an image like this:

Scaling an image

But what if you want to create a thumbnail and keep the original proportions? You will need to scale the image.

Image scaling is the process of changing the size of an image and saving the original proportions. If in the previous section, we manually picked the width and height, we will now calculate it.

Scaling by percentage

Let's start by scaling the image using percentages. Let's say we want to scale the image to be 60% of the original size:

```
using Images, ImageView
source_image = load("sample-images/cats-3061372_640.jpg");
scale_percentage = 0.6
new_size = trunc.(Int, size(source_image) .* scale_percentage)
resized_image = imresize(source_image, new_size)
imshow(resized_image);
```

We have done the following:

- We have loaded the image using the `load` function from the `Images` package
- We have defined the scaling percentage in the `scale_percentage` variable
- We have calculated the `new_size` by first multiplying the current size by our proportion and then converting the `float` values to `int`
- We have resized the image using the `new_size` values

The resulting image is neat and tidy. All of the proportions have been saved:

Don't forget that you can scale the image upward or downward if you so desire.

Scaling to a specific dimension

It is very common to scale your image to a given width and adapt the height automatically or vice versa.

There are multiple ways to approach this problem, but the most straightforward option would be to reuse and extend the code we wrote when scaling by percentage.

Given the original dimension and desired width, what would be the easiest way to calculate the change in percentage? That's correct—just divide the desired width or height by the original.

Let's assume we want to fix our width to 200 and calculate the value for `scale_percentage`:

```
new_width = 200
scale_percentage = new_width / size(source_image)[2]
```

Let's put it all together:

```
using Images, ImageView
source_image = load("sample-images/cats-3061372_640.jpg");
new_width = 200
scale_percentage = new_width / size(source_image)[2]
new_size = trunc.(Int, size(source_image) .* scale_percentage)
resized_image = imresize(source_image, new_size)
imshow(resized_image);
```

We have updated our scale by percentage solution to calculate `scale_percentage` dynamically based on a change in one of the dimensions.

Remember: `size(source_image)[1]` corresponds to height, while `size(source_image)[2]` corresponds to width.

Scaling by two-fold

This is a bonus section for scaling/resizing. The `JuliaImages` package has a very useful function called `somepkg(restrict)`, which reduces the size of an image by two-fold along the dimensions specified. In other words, it scales the image by 50%.

`restrict` can be run in three ways:

- Without an additional argument—the image will become twice as small in width and height
- Sending 1 as an argument will make the height twice as small
- Sending 2 as an argument will make the width twice as small

Let's run a demo. Try sending 1 as an additional argument so that we decrease the height by 50%:

Consider the following code:

```
using Images
source_image = load("sample-images/cats-3061372_640.jpg");
resized_image = restrict(source_image, 1); # height
imshow(resized_image);
```

Rotating images

Rotation is another must-know technique when working with any type of image. We will start by initializing the required libraries and loading the image from disk. We will also be using the CoordinateTransformations package from the JuliaImages collection to define a rotation transformation:

```
using Images, CoordinateTransformations
img = load("sample-images/cats-3061372_640.jpg");
tfm = LinearMap(RotMatrix(-pi/4))
img = warp(img, tfm)
imshow(img)
```

This results in the `img` variable being updated with a new image, which is shown as follows:

For ease of use, please refer to the following table:

Degree	Formula
-30°	-pi/6
-90°	-pi/2
180	pi

Please be aware that rotating by degrees other than 90°, -90°, and 180° will result in a black background being added around the original image.

Summary

In this chapter, you received your first introduction to the `JuliaImages` packages. We went through the process of loading images from disk and URL; performing a different set of transformations, such as resizing and scaling; and finally, learned how to save and preview results.

Next, we will focus on enhancing the image by improving the color scheme and removing noise.

Questions

Please answer the following questions to see whether you have successfully learned this chapter:

1. Which package(s) are required to load an image from a disk?
2. Which package is required to download a file from the internet?
3. Which types of files/file extensions are returned by the `readdir` function?
4. Which function is used to save an image to disk? What are the prerequisites for saving a file to disk?
5. What is the most noticeable difference when saving images in JPG or PNG formats?
6. What is the difference between `scale` and `resize`?

2
Image Enhancement

This chapter is all about working with image pixels, changing colors, and using the `ImageFiltering` package. We will learn how to update, convert an image to grayscale, improve color intensity, and we will learn what the linear and non-linear filtering operations are and how they can be used to transform images, such as sharpening, blurring, and smoothing.

In this chapter, we will cover the following topics:

- Accessing pixels
- Converting images into arrays of numbers
- Converting arrays of numbers into colors
- Changing color saturation
- Converting an image to grayscale
- Creating a custom color filter
- Padding images
- Blurring and sharpening images

Technical requirements

There are no any special requirements for this chapter, as long as you are following the book from Chapter 1, *Getting Started with JuliaImages*. If you have skipped the first chapter, please pay attention to the technical requirements there.

Images as arrays

`JuliaImages` are two-dimensional arrays, and every pixel can be either scalar or a one-dimensional array:

- Grayscale images represent pixels as scalar values and they are called `Gray`
- `RGB` is a three-dimensional array which represents each point in three different colors, such as red, green, and blue
- `PNG` images with a transparent background are called `RGBA`

Accessing pixels

When you use a `load` command in Julia, it reads the image and encodes it in `RGB`. In the following example, we will see how Julia manages information for a single pixel:

```
using Images
img = load("sample-images/cats-3061372_640.jpg")
img[1:1, 1:1, :]
```

After Julia executes the preceding set of commands, you should expect to see the following output:

```
julia> img[1:1, 1:1, :]
1×1×1 Array{RGB4{N0f8},3}:
[:, :, 1] =
 RGB4{N0f8}(0.349,0.282,0.212)
```

Pay attention to the last line. Our pixel is composed of an `RGB` object with `0.349,0.282,0.212` being the values corresponding to the values for each of the three channels.

You will also notice that the images are represented on a scale from 0 to 1:

- 0 represents black
- 1 represents white (saturated for `RGB`)

Floating points numbers are 8-bit integers scaled by 1/255. For example, white is represented as (1.0, 1.0, 1.0), black as (0, 0, 0), and gray as (0.5, 0.5, 0.5). It is not a very common representation for general use, such as replacing a specific color, but it is widely used as a result of the pre-processing step before using an image in neural networks.

Converting images into arrays of numbers

You may have already noticed that, in the previous example, when you load a colorful image in Julia, it is stored as a two-dimensional array of RGB4 objects. Let's look into it again in the following code:

```
julia> img[1:1, 1:1, :]
1×1×1 Array{RGB4{N0f8},3}:
[:, :, 1] =
 RGB4{N0f8}(0.349,0.282,0.212)
```

Everything is good unless you want to edit the content of a specific pixel. This is achieved by decomposing RGB4 into multiple channels using the channelview function, shown as follows:

```
using Images, ImageView
img = load("sample-images/cats-3061372_640.jpg")
img_channel_view = channelview(img)
img_channel_view
```

You should be able to see an output similar to the following in your Julia REPL:

```
julia> img_channel_view
3×360×640 ChannelView(::Array{RGB4{N0f8},2}) with element type
FixedPointNumbers.Normed{UInt8,8}:
[:, :, 1] =
 0.349N0f8 0.353N0f8 0.345N0f8 0.329N0f8 ...
```

Done! Now, every pixel is represented by three distinct values, and we can use a matrix operation to change the content of the pixels. Let's update all of the colors with a value over 0.7 so that they are 0.9:

```
using Images, ImageView
img = load("sample-images/cats-3061372_640.jpg")
img_channel_view = channelview(img)
img_channel_view[img_channel_view .> 0.7] = 0.9
imshow(img)
```

This will result in the background colors changing:

We will look into more complicated examples and create Instagram-like filters later in this chapter.

 Copyright notice: Pixabay provides images under CC0 Creative Commons. They are free for commercial use and no attributions are required.

Converting arrays of numbers into colors

In the following chapters, we will need to convert an array of numbers into colors. This is achieved with the `colorview` function. Let's look into the following code to generate a random three-dimensional array and turn it into an RGB image:

```
using Images, ImageView
random_img_array = rand(3, 8, 8); # channel, height, width
img = colorview(RGB, random_img_array);
imshow(img)
```

It is important to note that the channel dimension is first, followed by height, then width. If the channel dimension is not first, but last, for example, we should use the `permuteddimsview` or `permutedims` functions to put them in the correct order. This is shown in the following code:

```
using Images, ImageView
random_img_array = rand(40, 100, 3); # height, width, channel
img_perm = permuteddimsview(random_img_array, (3, 1, 2))
img = colorview(RGB, Float16.(img_perm))
imshow(img)
```

An alternative way of writing the same code is as follows:

```
using Images, ImageView
random_img_array = rand(40, 100, 3); # height, width, channel
img_perm = permutedims(random_img_array, [3, 1, 2])
img = colorview(RGB, img_perm)
imshow(img)
```

The difference in the two preceding options is the moment when we allocate memory. The first option allocates memory on `Float16` and the second option allocates on `permutedims`. We will be using both of these options for different scenarios.

Changing color saturation

Previously, you learned how to convert colors to multi-dimensional channels, and now we will learn how to change the content of a specific channel in the RGB color scheme to simulate filters from your favorite photo applications.

Let's start by simply loading an image of cats and following these steps:

1. We will convert the image of cats to `channelview`, and set the channels to be the last dimension, as follows:

```
using Images, ImageView
img = load("sample-images/cats-3061372_640.jpg");
img_ch_view = channelview(img); # extract channels
img_ch_view = permuteddimsview(img_ch_view, (2, 3, 1));
# reorder channels
```

2. We will split the existing image into two parts and use the second part to apply the filter, as follows:

```
x_coords = Int(size(img, 2) / 2):size(img, 2);
```

3. Let's start by simply increasing the saturation for the first channel by 10% and limiting it to a maximum of 1. This is done by multiplying the existing channel values by 1.1 in combination with the min function. Please also remember that the first channel corresponds to the color red:

```
img_ch_view[:, x_coords, 1] = min.(img_ch_view[:, x_coords, 1] .*
1.1, 1);
imshow(img)
```

4. You should be able to see an image of two cats with the second part of it being more of a red color. This is shown in the following image:

5. Let's proceed and update the second channel by increasing its saturation by 20%. The second layer corresponds to the color green:

```
img_ch_view[:, x_coords, 2] = min.(img_ch_view[:, x_coords, 2] .*
1.2, 1);
imshow(img)
```

Note that the image has changed and has become yellow. This happens when you mix red and green:

6. Now, let's also change the third channel, which corresponds to blue, and increase its intensity by 40%:

```
img_ch_view[:, x_coords, 3] = min.(img_ch_view[:, x_coords, 3] .*
1.4, 1);
imshow(img)
```

We managed to remove the colorful background and made the image look more realistic:

The final code block will look as follows:

```
using Images, ImageView
img = load("sample-images/cats-3061372_640.jpg");
img_ch_view = channelview(img);
img_ch_view = permuteddimsview(img_ch_view, (2, 3, 1));

x_coords = Int(size(img, 2) / 2):size(img, 2);

img_ch_view[:, x_coords, 1] = min.(img_ch_view[:, x_coords, 1] .* 1.1,
1);
img_ch_view[:, x_coords, 2] = min.(img_ch_view[:, x_coords, 2] .* 1.2,
1);
img_ch_view[:, x_coords, 3] = min.(img_ch_view[:, x_coords, 3] .* 1.4,
1);
imshow(img)
```

Keep in mind that the color scale is from 0.0 to 1.0 and other values are not accepted.

Notice that we did not allocate memory and used view to update the content of the original image.

Converting an image to grayscale

One of the most popular activities in computer vision is converting to and using a grayscale version of an image. In Julia, this is achieved by using the `Gray` function. This is shown as follows:

```
using Images
img = load("sample-images/cats-3061372_640.jpg");
img_gray = Gray.(img)
imshow(img_gray)
```

Grayscale images are widely used in classic computer vision, for tasks such as feature detection, morphology, and so on. The benefit of using grayscale images is that they are represented in a single dimension, which makes it fast for processing and analysis. We will be using this extensively throughout the book.

Keep in mind that `Gray` returns a single dimension, compared to three-dimensions for an `RGB` image. Use the following command to convert one channel `Gray` image to a three-channel grayscale `RGB` image:

```
img_gray_rgb = RGB.(Gray.(img_gray))
```

Creating a custom color filter

Would you like to create a more sophisticated filter and apply it to your images? We will put everything we have learned so far together to create a color-splash filter effect. The color-splash filter effect is achieved by using a spot or area representing the colors that are going to be retained. This is represented in the following image:

Let's start by loading an image. This time, we will use a Busan night scene from the `sample-images` folder. This provides us with a wide range of colors, and the splash effect will be prominent. We will load the image as follows:

```
using Images, ImageView

# load an image and create a grayscale copy
img = load("sample-images/busan-night-scene.jpg");
img_gray = RGB.(Gray.(img))
```

A few points to note here are the following:

- We create a grayscale copy of the image and use it as a basis for the final result
- We use a combination of `Gray` and `RGB` to get a three-channel representation for a grayscale version of the image

Let's proceed by representing the image objects in three channels using the `channelview` function. We will also change the order of the dimensions and put the channel dimension last. Consider the following code:

```
# get channels representation
img_channel_view = channelview(img);
img_gray_channel_view = channelview(img_gray);

# make channel dimension last and crop the required are
img_arr = permuteddimsview(img_channel_view, (2, 3, 1));
img_gray_arr = permuteddimsview(img_gray_channel_view, (2, 3, 1));
```

We will be using `mask` to keep track of the pixels and colors we want to keep. Initially, we set it to keep all the pixels:

```
# create a mask with all values being true
img_mask = fill(true, size(img));
```

Before proceeding with updating `mask`, we need to define a spot area in the original image. We will use the area to extract the colors we want to keep. You can change the value to anything as long as it fits the original area and previews it. This is done as follows:

```
# spot are with colors to retain
img_spot_height = 430:460
img_spot_width = 430:460

# preview color area (optional)
imshow(img[img_spot_height, img_spot_width])
```

The next part will be the most complicated. We will be executing multiple actions in one run. Consider doing the following:

1. Iterate over three channels of our image in a `for` loop and work on each one separately
2. Crop the area of interest from a channel
3. Identify the minimum and maximum color in the area
4. Create a channel mask by checking whether the channel color value falls within the minimum/maximum range
5. Apply the logical `AND` operation on image and channel masks

The code for the preceding actions is as follows:

```
for channel_id = 1:3

    # select current channel and crop areas of interest
    current_channel = view(img_arr, :, :, channel_id)
    current_channel_area = current_channel[img_spot_height,
     img_spot_width, :]

    # identify min and max values in a cropped area
    channel_min = minimum(current_channel_area)
    channel_max = maximum(current_channel_area)

    # merge existing mask with a channel specific mask
    channel_mask = channel_min .< current_channel .< channel_max
    img_mask = img_mask .& channel_mask
end
```

The final step is to apply `img_mask` and merge source image with grayscale:

```
img_masked = img_arr .* img_mask .+ img_gray_arr .* .~(img_mask);
final_image = colorview(RGB, permutedims(img_masked, (3, 1, 2)))
imshow(final_image)
```

Applying image filters

Now that you have learned how to apply changes to single pixels, it is time to learn about the `ImageFiltering.jl` package, which focuses on analyzing the information of neighborhood pixels and applying linear and non-linear filtering operations.

Padding images

At some point, you may want to add borders to the image. The `ImageFiltering` package extends the `padarray` function and allows you to add padding in different ways.

Padding with a constant value

Let's start with a simple scenario and add a 25-pixel border around the image. This is done by combining the `padarray` and `Fill` functions, as follows:

```
using Images, ImageView

pad_vertical = 25
pad_horizontal = 25
pad_color = RGB4{N0f8}(0.5,0.5,0.) # border color

img = load("sample-images/cats-3061372_640.jpg");
img = padarray(img, Fill(pad_color, (pad_vertical, pad_horizontal)))
img = parent(img) # reset indices to start from 1
imshow(img)
```

The resulting output is as follows:

padarray is using a custom index offset, which results in the first pixel starting from a number other than 1. parent is being used to reset the indices and starts them from 1.

Padding by duplicating content from an image

Sometimes, you might like to use the content of an image to create borders. Julia has four different types (styles) you can use when growing the border. These are mentioned in the following table:

Type	Description	Example
:replicate	The border pixels extend beyond the image boundaries	*UUUU - UVWXYZ - ZZZZ*
:circular	The border pixels wrap around	*WXYZ - UVWXYZ - UVWX*
:symmetric	The border pixels reflect relative to a position between pixels	*YXWV - UVWXYZ - YXWV*
:reflect	The border pixels reflect relative to the edge itself	*XWVU - UVWXYZ - ZYXW*

For example, using :reflect would copy or mirror the border pixels. This is shown in the following code:

```
using Images, ImageView

pad_vertical = 25
pad_horizontal = 25

img = load("sample-images/cats-3061372_640.jpg");
img = padarray(img, Pad(:reflect, pad_vertical, pad_horizontal))
img = parent(img) # reset indices to start from 1
imshow(img)
```

The resulting output is as follows:

I urge you to try other options to find other differences. It is as simple as changing `:reflect` to `:replicate` or any other option.

Blurring images

In image enhancement, a Gaussian blur is a widely used approach to reduce image details and achieve a blurring effect. It is a non-linear operation that varies across target pixels and areas.

In order to apply a Gaussian blur in Julia, we will be using the `Gaussian kernel` and `imfilter` function from the `ImageFiltering.jl` package. In the following code, we will blur the second half of the image and preview the difference:

```
using Images, ImageView
img = load("sample-images/cats-3061372_640.jpg");
img_area_range = 320:640
```

```
img_area = img[:, img_area_range]
img_area = imfilter(img_area, Kernel.gaussian(5))
img[:, img_area_range] = img_area

imshow(img)
```

The resulting output is as follows:

Julia's implementation of the Gaussian kernel takes a single value representing the area around the pixel and replaces the target pixel with the median value. The kernel size should be a positive integer, with 1 representing minimal smoothing.

In the following code, we will try to achieve an Instagram-like video effect when videos that don't fit into a box are increased in size and their borders are blurred. We will start by loading an image, creating top and bottom paddings, and, finally, blurring them:

```
using Images, ImageView

border_size = 50
gaussian_kernel_value = 10

img = load("sample-images/cats-3061372_640.jpg");
```

```
# add borders
img = padarray(img, Pad(:reflect, border_size, 0))
img = parent(img) # reset the indices after using padarray

# apply blurring to top border
img_area_top = 1:border_size
img[img_area_top, :] = imfilter(img[img_area_top, :],
Kernel.gaussian(gaussian_kernel_value))

# apply blurring to bottom border
img_area_bottom = size(img, 1)-border_size:size(img, 1)
img[img_area_bottom, :] = imfilter(img[img_area_bottom, :],
Kernel.gaussian(gaussian_kernel_value))

imshow(img)
```

The resulting image is as follows:

You can see that we used content nicely to enlarge the image and smoothen to get it to a size we want.

Sharpening images

We will be implementing an image sharpening technique used by modern graphical editors, such as GIMP and Photoshop. This suggests that we apply the Gaussian smoothing filter to a copy of an image and subtract the smoothed version from the original image (in a weighted way so that the values of a constant area remain constant).

Let's try to apply sharpening to our image of cats and see the change:

```
using Images, ImageView

gaussian_smoothing = 1
intensity = 1

# load an image and apply Gaussian smoothing filter
img = load("sample-images/cats-3061372_640.jpg");
imgb = imfilter(img, Kernel.gaussian(gaussian_smoothing));

# convert images to Float to perform mathematical operations
img_array = Float16.(channelview(img));
imgb_array = Float16.(channelview(imgb));

# create a sharpened version of our image and fix values from 0 to 1
sharpened = img_array .* (1 + intensity) .+ imgb_array .* (-intensity);
sharpened = max.(sharpened, 0);
sharpened = min.(sharpened, 1);
imshow(sharpened)

# optional part: comparison
img[:, 1:321] = img[:, 320:640];
img[:, 320:640] = colorview(RGB, sharpened)[:, 320:640];
imshow(img)
```

The resulting image is as follows:

Changing `gaussian_smoothing` to 2 makes it even more sharpened:

Feel free to play around with the `gaussian_smoothing` and `intensity` parameters to achieve the required outcome. `gaussian_smoothing` is recommended to be set from 1 to 4 and the `intensity` from 0.1 to 5.

Summary

This chapter was all about working with every pixel of an image. We have learned to work with different channels and adjust them to make colors more intense and to produce a color-splash effect. We have also looked into the `ImageFiltering` package and used it to create pads, blurring, and sharpened images.

In the next chapter, we will move on to working with the `ImageMorphology` package, which is used to separate objects, remove noise, and extend the background area.

Questions

1. What is the difference between `Gray` and `RGB` image representation?
2. When would you use the `channelview` function?
3. When would you use the `permuteddimsview` function?
4. What is the difference between using the `Fill` function and one of the border padding effects?
5. How did we achieve the image sharpening effect?

Image Adjustment 3

This chapter will guide you through the `ImageMorphology` package.

Morphological transformations are simple mathematical operations applied to a binary or grayscale image. They are used to remove small noise; shrink, separate, or identify an object; and increase the object size or background space.

The following topics will be covered in this chapter:

- Image erosion and dilation
- Image opening and image closing
- `Top-hat` and `bot-hat` operations
- Applying and combining techniques

Technical requirements

We will be using the `JuliaImages` and `ImageMorphology` packages throughout the chapter. Basic knowledge of the `JuliaImages` package is required.

Code samples are found on GitHub at `http://github.com/PacktPublishing/Hands-On-Computer-Vision-with-Julia/tree/master/Chapter03`.

We will be using a different set of images in this chapter. They can be downloaded from `https://pixabay.com` or downloaded from `http://juliaimages.github.io/TestImages.jl/`.

Image binarization

A core part of the `ImageMorphology` package is grayscale or binarized images. You have already learned how to create grayscale images. Binary images are those whose pixels are represented by either 1 or 0. Most of the examples you will find in this book and online have the following standard notation:

- 0 or black is used for the background
- 1 or white is used for the foreground, that is, our object

We will use the following code to create a binary image by a simple thresholding of a grayscale, that is, for example, assigning a 1 if the pixel value is over 0.5 and a 0 if it is below 0.5.

Binary and grayscale images are not perfect because they may contain numerous imperfections and are distorted by noise or texture. Morphological image transformations are targeted at removing these imperfections by using the form and structure of the image. These operations rely only on the relative ordering of the pixel values, not on their numerical values, and they are widely used to identify and process text, documents, and other shapes, such as lines and boxes.

The following code will demonstrate how to create a binary image with a threshold of 0.5. We will start by loading an image and applying a simple mathematical transformation to a grayscale version of the image:

```
using Images, ImageView, ImageMorphology

# load an image
img = load("sample-images/bird-3183441_640.jpg");

# convert image to grayscale and binarise the only channel
img_binary = 1 * (Gray.(img) .> 0.5);
```

A binary image one-liner executes three different operations:

- It converts the image to grayscale
- It converts all values over 0.5 to `true` and below 0.5 to `false`
- It converts `true` and `false` values to 1 or 0 by multiplying 1 by the result array

You can preview the original image in line with the binary version. This is achieved by following these steps:

1. Scale the original and binary images using the `restrict` function
2. Identify the width of a scaled version of the image using `size`
3. Create a new image, using the `fill` function, that is twice as large in width
4. Put the images in **step 1** together

Consider the following code:

```
# resize images by half for preview
img = restrict(img)
img_binary = restrict(RGB.(Gray.(img_binary)))

# stack 2 images together in line and preview
img_width = size(img, 2)
combined_image = fill(RGB4{Float32}(0.,0.,0.), size(img) .* (1, 2))
combined_image[:, 1:img_width] = img
combined_image[:, img_width+1:img_width*2] = img_binary
imshow(combined_image)
```

This will result in the original image being shown together with the binarized image. This time we are lucky, and there is no noise to remove and the contours are clear, as seen in the following photos:

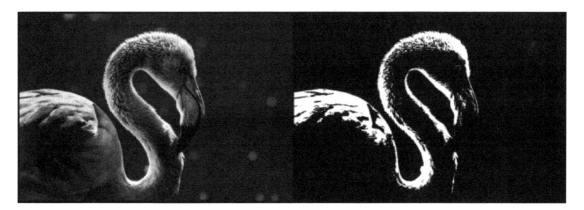

Morphological operations can also be applied to grayscale images so that their light transfer functions are unknown, and therefore their absolute pixel values are of no or little interest.

Fundamental operations

Mathematical morphology is a set of non-linear operations and techniques related to the shape or features of an image. There are two base elements of image morphology:

- A binary, or grayscale, image
- The structuring element

We have already discussed the prerequisites regarding image and color scheme, but the structuring element is new to us. The structuring element is usually a 3x3 binary block that slides over the image and updates it. There are two fundamental operations achieved by sliding the structuring element:

- **Image erosion**: Removes pixels from object boundaries
- **Image dilation**: Adds pixels to the borders of objects in an image

At the time of writing, `erode` and `dilate` from the `ImageMorphology` package support 3x3 structuring elements only. The 3x3 square is the most popular structuring element used in morphological operations. A larger structuring element creates a more extreme erosion or dilation effect although, usually, very similar results can be achieved by repeating the process many times.

Image erosion

Image erosion is one of the two base operators in the area of mathematical morphology. *Erosion* is a process of shrinking the image's foreground or 1-valued objects. It smoothes object boundaries and removes peninsulas, fingers, and small objects.

To understand the way image erosion works, we will first try it on a simple image containing white noise, and continue with comparing the results when applied to binary and grayscale versions of a photo.

Object separation using erosion

For this task, we will be using `geometrical-figures-and-noise.jpg` from the `sample-images` folder. It has many different connected figures and noise added on both sides:

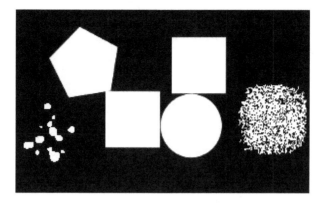

We will start by loading the image and converting it into grayscale, using the following code:

```
using Images, ImageView, ImageMorphology

geom_img = load("sample-images/geometrical-figures-and-noise.jpg");
geom_img_binary = Gray.(Gray.(geom_img) .< 0.5); # keeps white objects
white
```

Next, we will apply the `erode` function to see the transformation:

```
geom_img_binary_e = erode(geom_img_binary)
imshow(geom_img_binary_e)
```

The following resulting image will be shown on your screen. You should be able to see a considerable reduction in added noise and improved object separation:

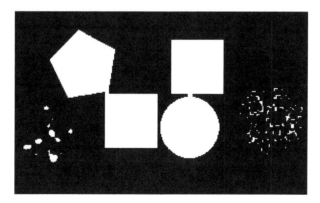

Unfortunately, running the `erode` function once did not entirely remove the noise, and it kept the objects connected. We will run the `erode` function three to five times to see whether having more rounds helps:

```
geom_img_binary_e = erode(erode(geom_img_binary_e))
imshow(geom_img_binary_e)

geom_img_binary_e = erode(erode(geom_img_binary_e))
imshow(geom_img_binary_e)
```

You should be able to see two more images on your screen. If the first image has a small amount of noise on the left, then the second one has no noise at all, and all objects should be well separated.

This is the first image:

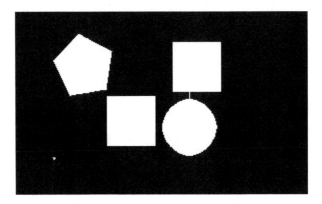

This is the second image:

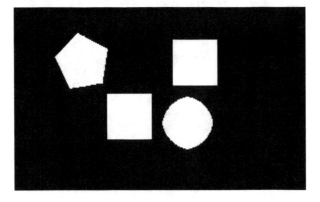

Image preparation for text recognition

You should have grasped the idea of how image erosion works on simple objects, and now we will continue with applying it to a real photo, separating a number plate's letters and digits from the rest of the content. Consider the following number plate:

The `caribbean-2726429_640.jpg` image is stored in the `sample-images` folder. We will first load the image, then create a binarized version, and then apply the `erode` function many times and compare the results, as follows:

```
using Images, ImageView, ImageMorphology
carplate_img = load("sample-images/caribbean-2726429_640.jpg")
carplate_img_binary = Gray.(Gray.(carplate_img) .< 0.5);
# converts black objects to white and vice-versa
carplate_img_binary_e = erode(carplate_img_binary)
imshow(carplate_img_binary)

carplate_img_binary_e = erode(erode(carplate_img_binary_e))
imshow(carplate_img_binary_e)
```

These are the results from eroding the image once and three times. No other text is left on the image, and the number plate is clear. Without any doubt, this can be used in text-recognition activities.

This is the first image:

This is the second image:

Image dilation

Dilation is the other fundamental operation in the area of mathematical morphology. **Image dilation** is the process of gradually enlarging the boundaries of regions of foreground pixels or the size of 1-valued objects. Thus, areas of foreground pixels grow in size, smoothing object boundaries and closing holes and gaps between objects.

To understand the way image dilation works in practice, we will use the same image with geometrical objects and a photo.

Merging almost-connected objects

As in the previous activities, we will be using `geometrical-figures-and-noise.jpg` from the `sample-images` folder. It has many different connected figures and noise added on both sides, as shown in the following screenshot:

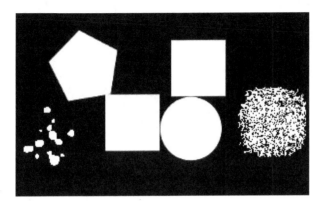

We will start by removing gaps and holes between geometrical objects and comparing when running the `dilate` function once and three times, by using this code:

```
using Images, ImageView, ImageMorphology

geom_img = load("sample-images/geometrical-figures-and-noise.jpg");
geom_img_binary = Gray.(1 * Gray.(geom_img) .> 0.5);
geom_img_binary_d = dilate(geom_img_binary)
imshow(geom_img_binary_d)

geom_img_binary_d = dilate(dilate(geom_img_binary_d))
imshow(geom_img_binary_d)
```

From the results shown in the following images, you can see that the overlap between figures increased a lot, and the noise on the right became a single object.

This is the first image:

This is the second image:

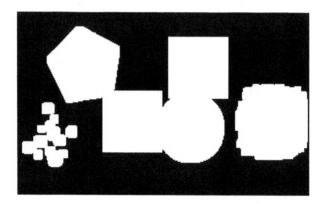

Highlighting details

Now we will try to apply the `dilate` function to an image with the number plate. If the `erode` function has been separating the number plate letters and digits, then `dilate` will extend the borders of every object. We will use the following code to implement this:

```
using Images, ImageView, ImageMorphology
carplate_img = load("sample-images/caribbean-2726429_640.jpg")
carplate_img_binary = Gray.(Gray.(carplate_img) .< 0.5)
carplate_img_binary_d = dilate(carplate_img_binary)
imshow(carplate_img_binary_d)
```

If you repeat code and zoom in the result, you will see that the borders of the map behind the digits are taking more space:

Derived operations

Opening and closing are the other two primary operators of mathematical morphology. They are both derived from the two base operations—**erosion** and **dilation**. Like those functions, they are normally used on binary or grayscale images.

From a technical perspective, opening and closing can be described in the following ways:

- Opening: This is the dilation of the erosion
- Closing: This is the erosion of the dilation

It is essential to note that erosion is not the inverse of dilation. In general, eroding and dilating produces an image different than the original, and identical results are created by chance.

As with base morphological operators, the exact operation is determined by a structuring element, which in Julia is fixed to a 3x3 block.

Image opening

Image opening is somewhat comparable to erosion. It is being applied to remove foreground pixels from the edges; however, it is less effective than erosion, in general.

Image opening is targeted at keeping foreground regions that have a similar shape to the structuring element or that can fully contain the structuring element while eliminating all other areas of foreground pixels.

To illustrate how it works in practice, we will use this image with geometrical figures and see how the opening is different than erosion:

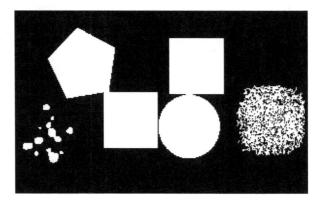

Let's get to the coding part and apply the opening function to the preceding image:

```
using Images, ImageView, ImageMorphology
geom_img = load("sample-images/geometrical-figures-and-noise.jpg");
geom_img_binary = Gray.(1 * Gray.(geom_img) .> 0.5);
geom_img_binary_o = opening(geom_img_binary)
imshow(geom_img_binary_e)
```

If you compare the results generated by opening and erode functions, you will see that opening (first image) has kept the large object untouched, and it has removed the small dots, when, at the same time, erode (second image) has reduced the size of all of the objects.

This is the first image:

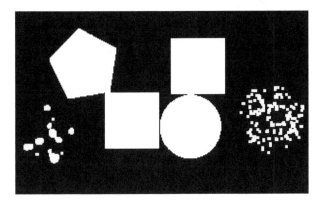

This is the second image:

Image closing

Image closing is the erosion of the dilation. Similar to `opening`, it is created from the base processes of erosion and dilation, and, the same as before, it can be applied both to binary and grayscale images.

The result of the `closing` operator is very similar to dilation, but with some exceptions. It is primarily focused on removing background color holes while being less disruptive to the original boundary shapes of the target objects.

Similar to image opening, we will use the image with geometrical figures and adjust the code the execute `closing` operation. Consider the following code:

```
using Images, ImageView, ImageMorphology
geom_img = load("sample-images/geometrical-figures-and-noise.jpg");
geom_img_binary = Gray.(Gray.(geom_img) .> 0.5);
geom_img_binary_c = closing(geom_img_binary)
imshow(geom_img_binary_c)
```

If you compare the image shown (first image) with the results from `dilation` (second image), you will see that the large objects did not grow in size and that a small area of the background became white.

This is the first image:

This is the second image:

Top-hat and bottom-hat operation

Have you ever been interested in getting some small details from an image? The Julia Morphology package also implements `tophat` and `bothat` operators focused on retrieving these kinds of details.

The `top-hat` filter is applied to enhance bright objects of interest on a dark background. It transforms an image by subtracting a result from running the `opening` function from the original image. It holds those elements of a source image that are smaller than the structuring element and are brighter than their neighbors.

The `bottom-hat` operation, on the other hand, is used to do the opposite; that is, it is used to enhance dark objects of interest on a bright background. The `bottom-hat` operator returns an image that is a result of subtracting the original image from a morphologically closed version of the image. The result contains objects or elements that are smaller than the structuring element, and are darker than their surroundings.

Julia implements `tophat` and `bothat` functions to achieve the functionality that we will be trying, using the following code to execute both filters on the image with geometrical figures, as seen in the preceding section. Here is our code:

```
using Images, ImageView, ImageMorphology

# apply tophat and bothat to an image
geom_img = load("sample-images/geometrical-figures-and-noise.jpg");
geom_img_gray = Gray.(geom_img);
geom_img_th = tophat(geom_img_gray)
geom_img_bh = bothat(geom_img_gray)

# create a preview
geom_img_new = zeros(ColorTypes.Gray{FixedPointNumbers.Normed{UInt8,8}},
size(geom_img_gray) .* (1, 2));
geom_img_new_center = Int(size(geom_img_gray, 2))

geom_img_new[:, 1:geom_img_new_center] = geom_img_th
geom_img_new[:, geom_img_new_center:end - 1] = geom_img_bh
geom_img_new[:, geom_img_new_center] = 1
imshow(Gray.(geom_img_new))
```

As you can see from the following result, the `tophat` function suppressed all large objects and kept only small details of the original image:

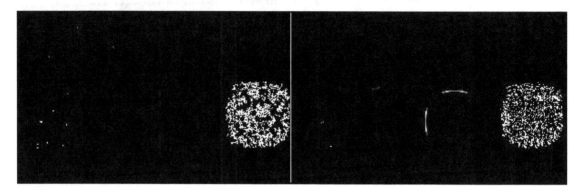

Adjusting image contrast

Adjustment of image contrast is possible on grayscale images by adding the original image to the `top-hat` filtered image and then subtracting the `bottom-hat` filtered image. We can do this by using the following code:

```
using Images, ImageView, ImageMorphology
minmax = scaleminmax(Gray, 0, 1) # limit values on a scale from 0 to 1

# adjust image contrast
img = load("sample-images/fabio_gray_512.png");
img_gray = Gray.(img);
img_new = minmax.(img_gray + tophat(img_gray) - bothat(img_gray))
# adjust image contrast

# merge the original image with adjusted for preview
img_center = Int(size(img_gray, 2) / 2)
img_gray[:, img_center:end] = img_new[:, img_center:end]
img_gray[:, img_center] = 0
imshow(img_gray)
```

In the preceding code, we have first defined the `minmax` function that limits the pixel values on a scale from 0 to 1. Aside from loading the image and converting it to grayscale, we have implemented the code part responsible for adjusting the contrast. The rest of the code is dedicated to creating the preview, displayed as follows:

Sometimes, using 100% value from the `tophat` and `bothat` functions has an enormous impact and distorts the image. We fix the distortion by minimizing the effect of the `tophat` and the `bothat` function using a multiplier on a scale from 0 to 1:

```
img = load("sample-images/busan-night-scene.jpg");
img_gray = Gray.(img);
img_new = minmax.(img_gray + tophat(img_gray) * 0.5 - bothat(img_gray) *
0.5)

img_center = Int(size(img_gray, 2) / 4)
img_gray[:, img_center:end] = img_new[:, img_center:end]
img_gray[:, img_center] = 0
imshow(img_gray)
```

You will see the original version on the left-hand side and an adjusted version on the right-hand side. There is a visible improvement in the quality of details on the right-hand side, as you can see from this photo:

Summary

In this chapter, you have learned how to apply a different set of techniques from the `ImageMorphology` package. These operations helped you to modify the original image and remove small noise; shrink, separate, and identify objects; and adjust background space.

These techniques are used as a preprocessing step before document processing, object detection, and tracking, which will be covered later in this book.

Now that you have learned how to adjust and enhance grayscale images, let's move on to partitioning colorful images using image segmentation techniques.

Questions

Please answer the following questions to confirm you understood the material:

1. What is a structuring element in the `ImageMorphology` package?
2. What is the size of structuring element blocks in Julia?
3. What are the prerequisites for the image color scheme before applying morphological processing?
4. What is the difference between the `erode` and the `dilate` functions?
5. What is the difference between the `erode` and the `opening` functions?
6. When would you use a combination of the `tophat` and `bothat` functions?

4
Image Segmentation

This chapter explores the `ImageSegmentation` package. You will learn how to use supervised and unsupervised methods to simplify or represent an image as something that is more meaningful and easy to analyze. Sometimes, image segmentation is called upon to be the first step in object identification in an image.

The following topics are covered in this chapter:

- Supervised image segmentation using seeded region growing
- Image segmentation using Felzenszwalb and fast scanning algorithms
- Small segment pruning

Technical requirements

We will be using the `JuliaImages` and `ImageSegmentation` packages throughout this chapter. Knowledge of the `JuliaImages` package and image processing techniques is required.

The code samples for this chapter can be found on GitHub at `http://github.com/PacktPublishing/Hands-On-Computer-Vision-with-Julia/tree/master/Chapter04`.

We will be using a different set of images in this chapter. You can acquire them from `https://pixabay.com`, download them from `http://juliaimages.github.io/TestImages.jl/`, or get from the other source specified.

Supervised methods

Image segmentation is the process of clustering or partitioning the pixels of an image into a set of regions corresponding to the individual surfaces, object, or parts of the object.

Medical image processing, object detection, face recognition, pedestrian detection, and satellite photo analysis incorporates image segmentation techniques. On top of that, image segmentation techniques can simplify and compress images in size.

There are two ways to approach the image segmentation problem—*supervised* and *unsupervised*, that is, by manually defining the number of segments and regions or letting the algorithm entirely do the job.

Seeded region growing

We will start with a supervised approach, an assisted way of solving a problem.

Identifying a simple object

In the following section, we will learn to separate a foreground object, which is a cat, from the rest of the background. For this, consider the following code:

```
using Images, ImageView, ImageSegmentation
img = load("sample-images/cat-3352842_640.jpg");
imshow(img)
```

Let's start by loading this image into Julia and previewing it:

Julia implements the `seeded_region_growing` function to achieve this task. The prerequisites for using the `seeded_region_growing` function are the following:

- An image
- A set of points specifying each region

The `seeded_region_growing` function requires us to supply the coordinates of the cat manually. The easiest option would be to hover the cursor over the cat and note down the coordinates from the bottom-left corner of the preview window, such as [220, 250]. We also need a value for the grass, such as [220, 500].

The `ImageSegmentation` package requires us to define all segments as an array of tuples of `CartesianIndex` along with a segment number. Consider the following code:

```
seeds = [
 (CartesianIndex(220,250), 1),
 (CartesianIndex(220,500), 2)
]
```

The moment `seeds` are defined, we will be calling the `seeded_region_growing` function, which assigns every pixel to a segment as follows:

```
segments = seeded_region_growing(img, seeds)
```

Now, we will use the `map` function to replace the segment number of each pixel with a mean color value of a segment:

```
imshow(map(i->segment_mean(segments,i), labels_map(segments)))
```

This results in an image consisting of two colors, with green representing grass and the other representing the cat. Because the image is relatively simple and the cat can be easily separated, the result is of a very high quality. This is shown in the following image:

Despite the fact that this approach involves manual work, it can be handy when preparing training datasets for image segmentation tasks executed by neural networks.

The image of the cat was taken from `https://pixabay.com/en/cat-british-longhair-breed-cat-3352842/`.

Identifying a complex object

Now, we will move on and try to separate or segment an object that cannot be easily separated from the background, or consists of multiple parts. This time, we will use an image of a bird, which we have seen before when learning about conversion to binary images:

Let's just run the code from the previous section and see whether it needs any improvements:

```
using Images, ImageView, ImageSegmentation
img = load("sample-images/bird-3183441_640.jpg");

seeds = [
  (CartesianIndex(220,250), 1), # apprx. object location
  (CartesianIndex(220,500), 2) # background location
]

segments = seeded_region_growing(img, seeds)
imshow(map(i->segment_mean(segments,i), labels_map(segments)))
```

From the following image, we can see that it did not end up the same way as with the image of the cat. The segmentation process could not fully separate the object:

The complexity is that the bird consists of multiple colors, which are similar to the background. Let's try to define more segments and see if this improves the result. The same as in the previous section, we hover over different areas of an image and note the coordinates. Consider the following code:

```
img = load("sample-images/bird-3183441_640.jpg");

seeds = [
  (CartesianIndex(240,120), 1),
  (CartesianIndex(295,70), 2),
  (CartesianIndex(319,40), 3),
  (CartesianIndex(90,300), 4),
  (CartesianIndex(295,325), 5),
  (CartesianIndex(76,135), 6) # background color
]

segments = seeded_region_growing(img, seeds)
imshow(map(i->segment_mean(segments,i), labels_map(segments)))
```

Defining more segments helped us to separate the object. We can also see how different the average color is in each of the segments, which vary from desert sand to black. See the following image:

The most significant disadvantage of this approach is that you have to define segments manually. Now, we will look into an unsupervised method that finds segments automatically.

Unsupervised methods

Unsupervised methods, on the other hand do not require you to mark the area or choose regions manually. The process of identifying segments is fully automatic, with some hyper-parameters available to set the minimum segment size and detail level.

The graph-based approach

This time, will be using the **Felzenszwalb** algorithm, which is an unsupervised and efficient graph-based approach. It was proposed by P.F Felzenszwalb and Huttenlocher in 2004 and has been actively used in computer vision since. The benefits of using the Felzenszwalb algorithm are as follows:

- A small number of hyperparameters
- Fast and linear execution time
- Preserves details in low variability areas

Julia implements Felzenszwalb algorithms in the `felzenszwalb` function, which is part of the `ImageSegmentation` package. `felzenszwalb` has two parameters:

- The threshold for the region merging step; the bigger the value, the larger the segment, which is usually set from 10 to 500
- Minimum (optional) segment size; usually 20 or higher

Depending on your task, the parameter values will change. Let's practice and see how different parameter values change the result. As always, we will start by loading the packages and the image:

```
using Images, ImageView, ImageSegmentation

img = load("sample-images/cat-3352842_640.jpg");
imshow(img);
```

We will be trying the Felzenszwalb algorithms with a threshold merging step value of 75 and we will compare its performance for different values of minimum segment size:

```
segments_1 = felzenszwalb(img, 75)
segments_2 = felzenszwalb(img, 75, 150)
segments_3 = felzenszwalb(img, 75, 350)
```

So, the values are calculated. The `segments_x` variables keep information on each pixel and its class.

As we will be comparing three different results of the Felzenszwalb algorithm, I thought it would be smart to move the conversion from segment codes to colors to a separate function:

```
segment_to_image(segments) = map(i->segment_mean(segments, i),
labels_map(segments))
```

Now, we are left with joining the results together and separating them with the black line:

```
img_width = size(img, 2)

new_img = hcat(
  segment_to_image(segments_1),
  segment_to_image(segments_2),
  segment_to_image(segments_3)
)

new_img[:, img_width] = new_img[:, img_width*2] = colorant"black"
imshow(new_img)
```

The preceding code example will generate a single image, which is a combination of three different runs of the algorithms, as follows:

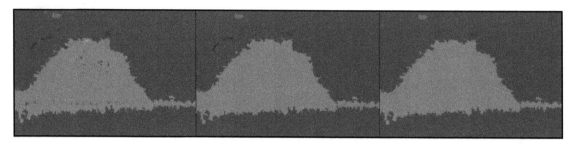

Although the algorithm did not perform as well as the *supervised* method, the results are still acceptable. You should also notice the number of details on the three different images. We managed to decrease the number of details on the second image and remove most of the foreground and background details in the third image by increasing the minimum segment size from none to 150 and 350 pixels.

Let's run the same code for the image of the bird and try different values for both parameters. In the following code example, we will be running the felzenszwalb function with the setups (10), (30, 50), and (35, 300), shown as follows:

```
# load an image
img = load("sample-images/bird-3183441_640.jpg");

# find segments
segments_1 = felzenszwalb(img, 10)
segments_2 = felzenszwalb(img, 30, 50)
segments_3 = felzenszwalb(img, 35, 300)

# the rest of the code from a previous example
...
```

The results are impressive. The first call separated the bird very well and kept most of the details of the image. Both the second and third versions are much-simplified versions of the original image, with the third image being reduced to only a few segments, thus selecting the foreground area very well, which is shown in the following image:

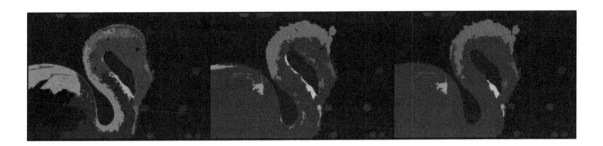

The fast scanning approach

The fast scanning algorithm is another unsupervised image segmentation algorithm. The fast scanning algorithm is efficiently used in food, sport, and medical images. It works by scanning pixels in the image and grouping neighboring pixels that are similar within a predefined threshold.

Julia implements fast scanning algorithms in the fast_scanning function, which is part of Julia's ImageSegmentation package. The fast_scanning function has three input parameters:

- **Image**: Color or grayscale
- **Threshold**: Float value or matrix in size of the image
- **diff_fn (optional)**: A custom function that calculates the difference

We will demonstrate the fast scanning algorithm on an identical example of the Felzenszwalb algorithm. We won't be discussing the code in detail, as most of it has been covered in the previous example. It is just important to pay attention to the calls we make to the fast_scanning function. We will use three different values for each segment: 0.05, .15, and 0.2. The higher the value, the smaller the number of segments that will be created and you will be able to see this in the end result. Consider the following code:

```
using Images, ImageView, ImageSegmentation

# convert image segments to mean color value
segment_to_image(segments) = map(i->segment_mean(segments, i),
labels_map(segments))
img = load("sample-images/cat-3352842_640.jpg");

# find segments
segments_1 = fast_scanning(img, 0.05)
segments_2 = fast_scanning(img, 0.15)
segments_3 = fast_scanning(img, 0.2)
```

```
# preview the results
img_width = size(img, 2)

new_img = hcat(
  segment_to_image(segments_1),
  segment_to_image(segments_2),
  segment_to_image(segments_3)
)

new_img[:, img_width] = new_img[:, img_width*2] = colorant"black"
imshow(new_img)
```

I haven't measured the function's execution time, but the algorithm performed much faster than the Felzenszwalb algorithm. The results also seem to have higher precision, which is shown as follows:

The only issue we have with the third image is that the fast scanning algorithm kept some of the small segments. We used the segment pruning technique, and similar to the seeded region growing algorithm, set a minimum segment size to 350 pixels.

The prune_segments function requires us to define two anonymous functions—one for identifying pixels of small segments and another to do the actual replacement. This is shown in the following code:

```
deletion_rule = i -> (segment_pixel_count(segments_3, i) < 350)
replacement_rule = (i, j) -> (-segment_pixel_count(segments_3, j))
segments_n = prune_segments(segments_3, deletion_rule, replacement_rule)

imshow(segment_to_image(segments_n))
```

Wow! The result is as good as the supervised method! No noise is left on the image and the cat is cropped really well:

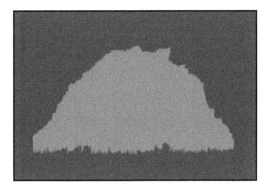

Let's move on to see and compare the algorithm's performance on the image of the bird:

```
# load an image
img = load("sample-images/bird-3183441_640.jpg");

# find segments
segments_1 = fast_scanning(img, 0.05)
segments_2 = fast_scanning(img, 0.15)
segments_3 = fast_scanning(img, 0.2)

# the rest of the code from a previous example
...
```

We can see that the algorithm did not perform at all. There are multiple reasons why it did not succeed, and the following two are the main reasons:

- Too many small details
- The foreground color is similar to the background color

Consider the following image:

We could apply pruning to the second image and see if merging the segments can solve the problem. Because the segments are already large in size, we will have to adjust the minimum segment size value as follows:

```
deletion_rule = i -> (segment_pixel_count(segments_2,i) < 750)
replacement_rule = (i,j) -> (-segment_pixel_count(segments_2, j))
segments_n = prune_segments(segments_2, deletion_rule, replacement_rule)

imshow(segment_to_image(segments_3))
```

The resulting number of segments is still high, but the image is very much simplified. I guess the target is achieved:

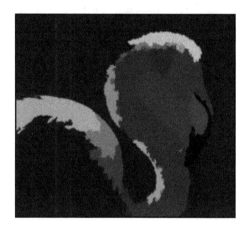

Helper functions

Let's assume we have the following code example, which is loading an image and running Felzenszwalb algorithms on an image:

```
using Images, ImageSegmentation
img = load("sample-images/cat-3352842_640.jpg");
segments = felzenszwalb(img, 75, 350)
```

What do you think is the output of the algorithm? Or in other words, what is stored in the segments variables? Let's check by typing segments in Julia REPL:

```
Main> segments
Segmented Image with:
 labels map: 426×640 Array{Int64,2}
 number of labels: 5
```

We see a well-formatted response, which does not expose any other information except the image size and number of labels or segments. In order to retrieve the information from the `segments` variable, we have been using the following set of functions:

- `labels_map`: An array of labels corresponding to every pixel of an image
- `segment_labels`: A list of all segment labels, either a number from 1 to N or a value you have set manually
- `segment_mean`: The mean intensity of the segment
- `segment_pixel_count`: The number of pixels from the image in the segment

You should be able to use the preceding functions with most of the algorithms from the Julia `ImageSegmentation` package.

A very good example of using all of these functions together is the `segment_to_image` function, which you may have seen and used before. It iterates over every pixel of an image, identifies its segment number, and converts it to the mean intensity of the segment. This is shown in the following code:

```
segment_to_image(segments) = map(i->segment_mean(segments, i),
labels_map(segments))
```

Summary

In this chapter, we have learned to simplify images and change their representation into something that is much easier to analyze, using a different set of algorithms available in the `ImageSegmentation` package. These algorithms include, but are not limited to, the seeded region growing technique, the Felzenszwalb algorithm, and the fast scanning algorithm. We have also learned how to use `helper` functions to extract additional information, such as retrieving segment labels, size, and mean intensity values.

In the next chapter, we will be looking at how to proceed with detailed feature extraction from images. This will be used in image grouping and comparison.

Questions

Please answer the following questions to confirm that you have understood the material:

1. What is the primary difference between seeded region growing and the fast scanning algorithm?
2. When would you use supervised image segmentation algorithms, such as the seeded region growing technique?
3. How does increasing and decreasing the threshold merging step parameter for the Felzenszwalb algorithm affect the results?
4. When would you use the segment pruning technique?

Further reading

We haven't covered many other image segmentation algorithms available in the `ImageSegmentation` package. You are welcome to investigate the mean shift and watershed algorithm on your own, for example, from another great book that's available:

- OpenCV 3 Computer Vision with Python Cookbook:
  https://www.packtpub.com/application-development/opencv-3-computer-vision-python-cookbook

5
Image Representation

The `ImageFeatures` package is used to determine features or descriptors of an image or its area and is later used in a different set of applications, such as object recognition, detection, image matching, and overlaying.

The following topics will be covered in this chapter:

- Corner detection using the FAST algorithm
- Corner detection using the `imcorner` function
- The BRIEF algorithm
- ORB, the rotation invariant algorithm
- The BRISK, rotation, and scale invariant algorithms

Technical requirements

We will be using the `JuliaImages`, `ImageFeatures`, and `BenchmarkTools` packages throughout the chapter. Knowledge of the `JuliaImages` package and image processing techniques is required.

Code samples are available on GitHub at `http://github.com/PacktPublishing/Hands-On-Computer-Vision-with-Julia/tree/master/Chapter05`.

Understanding features and descriptors

By the end of this chapter, you will understand what features are and learn to apply them in computer vision applications. Look at the following image and think about how you would solve a similar puzzle:

Most probably, you would search for patterns or specific features that are unique to the neighboring elements. Image features work similarly by representing the image in a set of parameters making them readily identified, tracked, and compared.

Let's look at two different images of cats and try finding the areas that match those images:

It seems to me that ears and eyes are common for both cats. Let's see what would one of the algorithms we will learn later in the chapter would do to the following image:

From the preceding result, you can see that the algorithm focused on the cats' ears, and this is represented by white lines that are connecting identical features.

FAST corner detection

Corner detection is the process of extracting features from an image.

The JuliaFeatures package implements **Features from accelerated segment test** (**FAST**). FAST is a computationally efficient corner detector and is suitable for real-time video analysis and a processing algorithm proposed by Edward Rosten and Tom Drummond. You can call the FAST algorithm by using the fastcorners function.

Because of its outstanding performance, quality, and simple configuration, we will be using FAST in all of the following examples. FAST works by scanning the entire image for object corners. It uses a circle of 16 pixels to evaluate whether a point is a corner. The process is also configured by two additional parameters:

- The number of contiguous pixels (*N)*
- The threshold value

The *number of contiguous pixels (N)* is used to compare whether the pixels in the circle are brighter or darker than the candidate point. *N* is usually fixed to 12, and the threshold value from 0.05 to X defines the number of features identified. The higher the value you set for a threshold parameter, the fewer features will get returned.

Let's try rerunning the FAST algorithm on one of the images of a cat, which was used earlier to see how the number of corners changes with a different value for a threshold parameter.

We will load the image, resize, and convert it to grayscale. We will also apply the `fastcorners` function with three different sets of threshold values, such as 0.15, 0.25, and 0.35, and compare the results. The code for it is as follows:

```
using Images, ImageFeatures

img = Gray.(load("sample-images/cat-3417184_640.jpg"))
img_f = Float16.(restrict(img))

new_img = Gray.(hcat(
  img_f .* (~fastcorners(img_f, 12, 0.15)),
  img_f .* (~fastcorners(img_f, 12, 0.25)),
  img_f .* (~fastcorners(img_f, 12, 0.35))
))

imshow(new_img)
```

The trick we used in the preceding code when we multiplied the numeric representation of an image stored in the `img_f` variable by a negation of the result, the `fastcorners` function, allows us to place features on an image quickly. The result of running the code is shown in the following images:

You should be able to see black dots on the cat. Those dots represent corners identified by the `fastcorners` function. They are used by other algorithms to match identical objects. You should be able to see black dots around the cat. Those dots represent corners identified by FAST. They are used by other algorithms to match identical objects or parts of the area.

In case of processing images with text, FAST can help you to identify areas that contain content. This is shown in the following code:

```
using Images, ImageFeatures

img = Gray.(load("sample-images/newspaper-37782_640.png"))
img_f = Float16.(img)
```

```
new_img = Gray.(hcat(
  img_f,
  Float16.(img_f) .* (~fastcorners(img_f, 12, 0.15))
))

imshow(new_img)
```

In the following image, you can see the comparison between the original image and a single run of FAST with a threshold of `0.15`. The black dots are all over the letters:

Let's move on and see how the results from FAST can be used to match images.

Corner detection using the imcorner function

The `imcorner` function is an alternative to FAST's `fastcorners`. It is also used on corners from an image and provides a different set of methods, such as the following ones:

- `harris`
- `shi-tomasi`
- `kitchen-rosenfield`

Each method performs in its own unique way, and therefore feature representation will differ. To better understand the differences, we will plot them all on a single image. Let's start by loading an image of a chessboard and converting it to a float representation, as shown in the following code:

```
using Images, ImageFeatures, ImageMorphology, ImageView

img = restrict(load("sample-images/board-157165_640.png"))
img_f = Float16.(Gray.(img))
```

Next, we will be running four different methods and algorithms; three of them will be provided by the `imcorner` function, and the last will be FAST. We are using FAST for comparison reasons. Consider the following code:

```
img_harris = copy(img)
img_harris[dilate(imcorner(img_f, method=harris)) .> 0.01] =
colorant"yellow"

img_shi = copy(img)
img_shi[dilate(imcorner(img_f, method=shi_tomasi)) .> 0.01] =
colorant"yellow"

img_rosenfield = copy(img)
img_rosenfield[dilate(imcorner(img_f, method=kitchen_rosenfeld)) .> 0.01] =
colorant"yellow"

img_fast = copy(img)
img_fast[dilate(fastcorners(img_f, 12, 0.05)) .> 0.01] = colorant"yellow"
```

Usually, the outcome of the `imcorner` and `fastcorners` functions are of a small size, such as one pixel. We have applied dilation from the `ImageMorphology` package to highlight the results identified by `imcorner` or FAST. It is an optional step and is done to have a better representation of features when they are plotted and previewed by the user. We have also used the `colorant` technique to get the precise color value.

Next, we combine all four images into a single image. On the top, you will find `harris` and `shi-tomasi`, and later you will find `kitchen-Rosenfield` and FAST:

```
new_img = vcat(
 hcat(img_harris, img_shi),
 hcat(img_rosenfield, img_fast)
 )
```

We will separate the images with a yellow line for a better representation and preview the results using the following code:

```
new_img[Int(size(new_img, 1) / 2), :] = colorant"yellow"
new_img[:, Int(size(new_img, 2) / 2)] = colorant"yellow"

imshow(new_img)
```

The output is as follows:

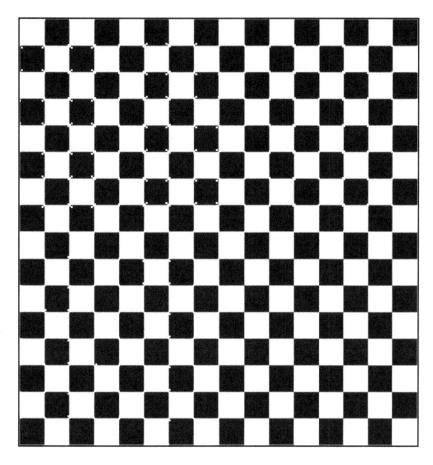

The results are very different. For example, `harris` (top-left) has many different corners compared to FAST (bottom-right), which does not have any. `Shi-tomas` and `kitchen_rosenfeld` are also very different than each other.

Let's try running identical code on an image of a cat and compare the results again to see whether anything changes:

```
using Images, ImageFeatures, ImageMorphology, ImageView

img = Gray.(restrict(load("sample-images/cat-3417184_640.jpg")))
img_f = Float16.(Gray.(img))

img_harris = copy(img)
img_harris[dilate(imcorner(img_f, method=harris)) .> 0.01] =
colorant"yellow"

img_shi = copy(img)
img_shi[dilate(imcorner(img_f, method=shi_tomasi)) .> 0.01] =
colorant"yellow"

img_rosenfield = copy(img)
img_rosenfield[dilate(imcorner(img_f, method=kitchen_rosenfeld)) .> 0.01] =
colorant"yellow"

img_fast = copy(img)
img_fast[dilate(fastcorners(img_f, 12, 0.05)) .> 0.01] = colorant"yellow"

new_img = vcat(
 hcat(img_harris, img_shi),
 hcat(img_rosenfield,img_fast)
)
imshow(new_img)
```

The results are very unexpected! All of the methods except FAST have corners all around the image. The reason for this is that the `imcorner` function returns all corners without any threshold parameter. Consider the following image:

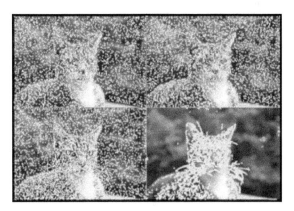

Let's update the threshold to retrieve only the top 5% of features and compare the results again:

```
img = Gray.(restrict(load("sample-images/cat-3417184_640.jpg")))
img_f = Float16.(Gray.(img))

img_harris = copy(img)
img_harris[dilate(imcorner(img_f, Percentile(95), method=harris)) .> 0.01]
= colorant"yellow"

img_shi = copy(img)
img_shi[dilate(imcorner(img_f, Percentile(95), method=shi_tomasi)) .> 0.01]
= colorant"yellow"

img_rosenfield = copy(img)
img_rosenfield[dilate(imcorner(img_f, Percentile(95),
method=kitchen_rosenfeld)) .> 0.01] = colorant"yellow"

img_fast = copy(img)
img_fast[dilate(fastcorners(img_f, 12, 0.05)) .> 0.01] = colorant"yellow"

new_img = vcat(
  hcat(img_harris, img_shi),
  hcat(img_rosenfield, img_fast)
)
imshow(new_img)
```

As you can see from the following image, the images have changed:

Great! This time the results are very similar!

Comparing performance

It is also important to run a performance comparison to see which of the algorithms and methods works faster. To run the analysis, I have used the `@btime` macro from the `BenchmarkTools` package in the following code:

```
using Images, ImageFeatures, BenchmarkTools

@btime fastcorners(img_f, 12, 0.15);
# Main> 6.504 ms (12 allocations: 150.27 KiB)

@btime fastcorners(img_f, 12, 0.05);
# Main> 8.954 ms (12 allocations: 150.27 KiB)

@btime imcorner(img_f, method=harris);
# Main> 8.022 ms (69574 allocations: 8.79 MiB)

@btime imcorner(img_f, Percentile(95), method=harris);
# Main> 7.024 ms (69574 allocations: 9.15 MiB)

@btime imcorner(img_f, method=shi_tomasi);
# Main> 8.133 ms (8986 allocations: 7.96 MiB)

@btime imcorner(img_f, method=kitchen_rosenfeld);
# Main> 7.122 ms (977 allocations: 7.25 MiB)
```

Despite the time growth for the smaller threshold value when using the `fastcorners` function, the memory consumption stays small and fixed. It makes it preferred algorithm for all subsequent tasks we will be doing in the following sections.

BRIEF – efficient duplicate detection method

Binary Robust Independent Elementary Features (**BRIEF**) is the first binary, but still efficient, feature point descriptor. BRIEF is an extremely simple feature descriptor and therefore cannot be applied to scaled or rotated images. Despite its limitations, it can be efficiently used for tasks such as duplicate detection.

Identifying image duplicates

In the following activities, we will be comparing an original image of a cat to a slightly modified and watermarked version of it.

Let's start by loading the image and converting it to a grayscale version, using the following code:

```
using Images, ImageFeatures, ImageDraw, ImageView
img1 = Gray.(load("sample-images/cat-3417184_640.jpg"))
img2 = Gray.(load("sample-images/cat-3417184_640_watermarked.jpg"))
imshow(restrict(hcat(img1, img2)))
```

We are also previewing the image to get an understanding of what we will be working with, as you can see from this image:

Next, we will use the `fastcorners` function to retrieve the keypoints or corner points and compare their counts from each of the images. We will decrease the number of keypoints returned, by using a high value for a threshold parameter when calling for `fastcorners`, as you can see from the following code:

```
keypoints_1 = Keypoints(fastcorners(img1, 12, 0.5));
# 0.5 - very high threshold
keypoints_2 = Keypoints(fastcorners(img2, 12, 0.5));

size(keypoints_1) # result varies from 190 to 200
size(keypoints_2) # result varies from 190 to 200
```

The number of parameters is very close, 190 versus 200. The next step would be to initialize BRIEF and call the `create_descriptor` function to create features. We will also be calling the `match_keypoints` function to match the results from both images, as shown in the following code:

```
brief_params = BRIEF()
desc_1, ret_features_1 = create_descriptor(img1, keypoints_1,
brief_params);
```

```
desc_2, ret_features_2 = create_descriptor(img2, keypoints_2,
brief_params);
matches = match_keypoints(ret_features_1, ret_features_2, desc_1, desc_2,
0.5)
```

The matches variable should return the number of matches between features. Running size will show us the count, as shown in the following code:

```
size(matches) # returns (199,)
```

So, the number of matches is 199, very good! Let's preview the results to confirm everything is correct. We will do this by merging two images and drawing a white line connecting the matches, as shown in the following code:

```
grid = hcat(img1, img2)
offset = CartesianIndex(0, size(img1, 2))
map(m -> draw!(grid, LineSegment(m[1], m[2] + offset)), matches)
imshow(grid)
```

Despite the changes to the image, we can see that the primary features were matched correctly. The process worked relatively fast, and well! Just take a look at the following images:

 If you ever decide to run duplicate detection on a much larger scale, then consider saving the results of create_descriptor in some kind of database. So, when the new image appears, you only need to compare it to the already precalculated features.

Because BRIEF is using only information for a single pixel, it makes it sensitive to noise. To overcome this limitation, it applies Gaussian blurring, which can be configured when initializing BRIEF.

Creating a panorama from many images

Another interesting activity you can perform using BRIEF or any of the other methods described in the following section is panoramic view creation. Let's assume you have many images of a sample place and you would like to connect them together and make one single result. We can try using BRIEF to connect the images based on their common features.

As always, let's start by loading the image of a cat into Julia and splitting it into two parts we will be trying to connect afterward. This requires us to define additional parameters, such as the width of the two new images. We will use the following code for this task:

```
using Images, ImageFeatures, ImageDraw, ImageShow
img = load("sample-images/cat-3418815_640.jpg")

img_width = size(img, 2)
img_left_width = 400
img_right_width = 340
```

Next, let's create two new images using the preceding settings. We will keep both the original and the grayscale versions. The grayscale version will be used to find the keypoints, and the color version will be used to create the final result. Take a look at this code:

```
img_left = view(img, :, 1:img_left_width)
img_left_gray = Gray.(img_left)
img_right = view(img, :, (img_width - img_right_width):img_width)
img_right_gray = Gray.(img_right)

imshow(img_left)
imshow(img_right)
```

The following images are our two new images we will be trying to connect next:

So, let's find the keypoints from the results of a `fastcorners` function, by using this code:

```
keypoints_1 = Keypoints(fastcorners(img_left_gray, 12, 0.3));
keypoints_2 = Keypoints(fastcorners(img_right_gray, 12, 0.3));
```

Now it is time to initialize BRIEF and find the matches between the features, using this code:

```
brief_params = BRIEF()
desc_1, ret_features_1 = create_descriptor(img_left_gray, keypoints_1,
brief_params);
desc_2, ret_features_2 = create_descriptor(img_right_gray, keypoints_2,
brief_params);
matches = match_keypoints(ret_features_1, ret_features_2, desc_1, desc_2,
0.1)
```

We can preview the results to see whether the keypoints were matched correctly by using this code:

```
grid = hcat(img_left, img_right)
offset = CartesianIndex(0, size(img_left_gray, 2))
map(m -> draw!(grid, LineSegment(m[1], m[2] + offset)), matches)
imshow(grid)
```

From the following image, you can see lots of different connections. I deliberately kept the number of features high to show different mismatches:

So, what should we do next? Let's assume that most of the points are identified correctly. If so, we can calculate the distance between each of the pairs of keypoints and find the median value that will represent the true value and will call it an offset. Take a look at this code:

```
offset_x = mean(map(m -> (img_left_width - m[1][2]) + m[2][2], matches))
```

To simplify the remaining steps, we divide the offset by half and reduce both images for the resulting value. Finally, we preview the outcome in line with the original image:

```
offset_x_half = Int(trunc(diff_on_x / 2))
img_output = hcat(
  img_left[:, 1:(img_left_width-offset_x_half)],
  img_right[:, offset_x_half:img_right_width]
)

imshow(hcat(img, img_output))
```

Great work! As you can see from this image, it is very hard to tell the difference between the two images!

ORB, rotation invariant image matching

The ORB descriptor is an improved version of BRIEF; it is a mix of a FAST keypoint detector combined with a modified and enhanced version of BRIEF.

A huge benefit of using ORB over BRIEF is the use of the `harris` corner measure that is built into ORB. It gives an opportunity to select top *N* uncorrelated keypoints. On top of that, the descriptor itself is enhanced and is rotation invariant.

We not only explore ORB by using a similar example, as in the previous section, but also apply rotation to the second image. We also use the CoordinateTransformations package to rotate the image around the center, as shown in the following code:

```
using Images, ImageFeatures, CoordinateTransformations

img1 = Gray.(load("sample-images/cat-3417184_640.jpg"))
img2 = Gray.(load("sample-images/cat-3417184_640_watermarked.jpg"))
```

Since the images are loaded, and we want to see whether ORB is rotation invariant, we apply warp transformation to img2 and rotate it around the center by using this code:

```
rot = recenter(RotMatrix(5pi/6), [size(img2)...] .÷ 2)
tform = rot ∘ Translation(-50, -40)
img2 = warp(img2, tform, indices(img2))
```

Next, we initialize ORB with a default set of parameters. The default setup creates a set of 500 keypoints and uses FAST with a threshold value of 0.25. The default setup should be fine for most of the tasks you ever run. Take a look at this code:

```
orb_params = ORB()
```

Because ORB uses FAST out of the box, we proceed directly to the create_descriptor function to create the image features and try to match them by using this code:

```
desc_1, ret_keypoints_1 = create_descriptor(img1, orb_params)
desc_2, ret_keypoints_2 = create_descriptor(img2, orb_params)

matches = match_keypoints(ret_keypoints_1, ret_keypoints_2, desc_1, desc_2,
0.2)
```

Now we can try to combine the images and preview the result, which can be done using this code:

```
grid = Gray.(hcat(img1, img2))
offset = CartesianIndex(0, size(img1, 2))
map(m -> draw!(grid, LineSegment(m[1], m[2] + offset)), matches)
imshow(grid)
```

Great! Despite the fact that the image has been rotated, ORB was able to match a number of primary keypoints from both images! Take a look at these images:

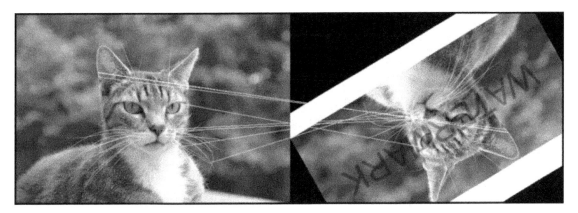

BRISK – scale invariant image matching

BRISK is another detector available in Julia. The most significant benefit of BRISK is that it is scale and rotation invariant. Scale invariance comes with computational costs, which makes it slightly slower than ORB.

BRISK also allows using any other keypoints descriptor provided by, for example, `imcorner`, such as `harris`. We continue using FAST as in the preceding examples.

So, let's start using BRISK. As always, we start by loading the packages and images, as shown in the following code:

```
using Images, ImageFeatures, CoordinateTransformations, ImageDraw,
ImageView

img1 = Gray.(load("sample-images/cat-3417184_640.jpg"))
img2 = Gray.(load("sample-images/cat-3417184_640_watermarked.jpg"))
```

We have set the target to demonstrate that BRISK is scale and rotation invariant. Then, we apply two types of transformations to `img2`, rotation around the center and resizing the image, by using this code:

```
rot = recenter(RotMatrix(5pi/6), [size(img2)...] .÷ 2)
tform = rot ∘ Translation(-50, -40)
img2 = warp(img2, tform, indices(img2))
img2 = imresize(img2, Int.(trunc.(size(img2) .* 0.7)))
```

As previously agreed, similar to BRIEF, we apply the FAST algorithm to find corners. We use a threshold value of 0.25, as shown in the following code:

```
features_1 = Features(fastcorners(img1, 12, 0.25));
features_2 = Features(fastcorners(img2, 12, 0.25));
```

Next, we initialize BRISK with default parameters and try to match the keypoints by using this code:

```
brisk_params = BRISK()
desc_1, ret_features_1 = create_descriptor(img1, features_1, brisk_params);
desc_2, ret_features_2 = create_descriptor(img2, features_2, brisk_params);
matches = match_keypoints(Keypoints(ret_features_1),
Keypoints(ret_features_2), desc_1, desc_2, 0.2)
```

The results are ready, and they are stored in the `matches` variable. We haven't discussed this before, but the `matches` variable is an array of two elements, each corresponding to a position on one of the images.

Since we want to display the results as a single image, we need to adjust the height of `img2` to be equal to the height of `img1` by using this code:

```
img3 = zeros(Gray, size(img1))
img3[1:size(img2, 1), 1:size(img2, 2)] = img2
```

We are left with drawing the lines connecting the matches. We use the `draw!` function from the `ImageDraw` package and display the result using the `imshow` function by using this code:

```
grid = hcat(img1, img3)
offset = CartesianIndex(0, size(img1, 2))
map(m -> draw!(grid, LineSegment(m[1], m[2] + offset)), matches)
imshow(grid)
```

As you can see from this image, the result is perfect. BRISK has successfully identified and matched features of the scaled and rotated image:

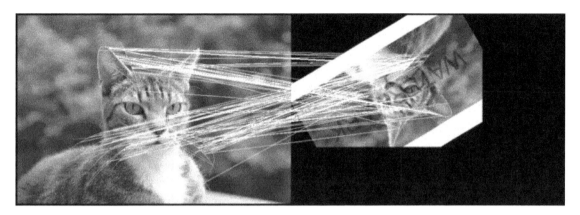

FREAK – fastest scale and rotation invariant matching

The last descriptor available in Julia is the FREAK descriptor, which was developed in 2012. The algorithm introduces a new keypoint descriptor inspired by the human visual system and, more precisely, the retina, coined the **Fast Retina Keypoint** (**FREAK**).

FREAKs are in general quicker to calculate with lower computational requirements. It makes them a great alternative to the methods covered in the preceding section. FREAK is considered to be the fastest scale, rotation, and noise invariant algorithm.

The code examples stay very similar to those we have already seen. First, we load the packages and images by using the following code:

```
using Images, ImageFeatures, CoordinateTransformations, ImageDraw,
ImageView

img1 = Gray.(load("cat-3417184_640.jpg"))
img2 = Gray.(load("cat-3417184_640_watermarked.jpg"))
```

We apply multiple transformations to the second image to complicate the example. We add rotation around the center and resize the image by using this code:

```
rot = recenter(RotMatrix(5pi/6), [size(img2)...] .÷ 2)
tform = rot ∘ Translation(-50, -40)
img2 = warp(img2, tform, indices(img2))
img2 = imresize(img2, Int.(trunc.(size(img2) .* 0.7)))
```

We execute the FAST algorithm to find the corners and use FREAK to match the keypoints by using this code:

```
keypoints_1 = Keypoints(fastcorners(img1, 12, 0.35));
keypoints_2 = Keypoints(fastcorners(img2, 12, 0.35));
freak_params = FREAK()
desc_1, ret_keypoints_1 = create_descriptor(img1, keypoints_1,
freak_params);
desc_2, ret_keypoints_2 = create_descriptor(img2, keypoints_2,
freak_params);
matches = match_keypoints(ret_keypoints_1, ret_keypoints_2, desc_1, desc_2,
0.2)
```

Similar to the preceding cases, we plot the results and generate a preview by using this code:

```
img3 = zeros(size(img1, 1), size(img2, 2))
img3[1:size(img2, 1), 1:size(img2, 2)] = img2

grid = Gray.(hcat(img1, img3))
offset = CartesianIndex(0, size(img1, 2))
map(m -> draw!(grid, LineSegment(m[1], m[2] + offset)), matches)
grid
```

As you can see from this image, the result is very nice:

The keypoints are matched very well. This seems very similar to BRISK.

Running face recognition

The last topic I would like to cover in the chapter is trying to match different images of the same person, to see whether we can build a face recognition model based on FREAK.

I have taken two images of a young woman and cropped the area around her face, assuming this would be the output from a camera. This is the image:

Let's proceed to the Julia code and run the images there, using this code:

```
using Images, ImageFeatures, ImageDraw, ImageView

img1 = Gray.(load("sample-images/beautiful-1274051_640_100_1.jpg"))
img2 = Gray.(load("sample-images/beautiful-1274056_640_100_2.jpg"))
```

Next, we find the keypoints and match them together with the help of FREAK by using this code:

```
keypoints_1 = Keypoints(fastcorners(img1, 12, 0.25));
keypoints_2 = Keypoints(fastcorners(img2, 12, 0.25));

freak_params = FREAK()
desc_1, ret_keypoints_1 = create_descriptor(img1, keypoints_1,
freak_params);
desc_2, ret_keypoints_2 = create_descriptor(img2, keypoints_2,
freak_params);
matches = match_keypoints(ret_keypoints_1, ret_keypoints_2, desc_1, desc_2,
0.2)
```

The moment the keypoints are matched, we can plot the results using the `ImageDraw` package by using this code:

```
grid = Gray.(hcat(img1, img2))
offset = CartesianIndex(0, size(img1, 2))
map(m -> draw!(grid, LineSegment(m[1], m[2] + offset)), matches)
imshow(grid)
```

The results are disappointing. The algorithm could not handle the different images of the same person, and I would not try running the face-recognition system using the preceding methods because of the low quality. There is no doubt we can spend more time on image adjustment, but the main question is this: is it worth it? Take a look at these images:

Summary

In this chapter, we have covered the process of simple object detection, duplicate checking, and image matching through a two-step process of feature extraction and descriptor matching. We have practiced and extracted image features using FAST, a corner detection algorithm, and subsequently applied feature descriptors such as BRIEF, ORB, and BRISK to create and match keypoints.

Next, we proceeded with using the keypoints of the images in machine learning activities, such as clustering and classification.

Later on in this book, we will learn to achieve this by using neural networks.

Questions

Please answer the following questions:

1. What is the purpose of corner detection?
2. How can corner detection help to identify areas with text?
3. How does the increase of the threshold value for FAST affect the number of features?
4. When would you use a BRIEF algorithm, and when would you use a BRISK one?
5. What is the primary difference between an ORB algorithm and BRISK?
6. Which of the three algorithms (BRIEF, ORB, and BRISK) implements FAST out of the box?

Introduction to Neural Networks

6

This chapter will primarily focus on understanding the difference between classic computer vision and neural networks, and also shows how to prepare images for use in deep learning models, and assist in building and training your first classifiers.

The following topics are covered in this chapter:

- Introduction to MXNet and its building blocks
- Building a digit classifier for the MNIST dataset
- Building a multiclass image classifier with CIFAR-10
- Building the cats and dogs classifier
- Reusing the models

Technical requirements

Users are required to have prior knowledge of Julia, but no previous knowledge of math or statistics is required.

Users are required to have the MLDatasets.jl, MXNet, and MXNet.jl packages installed. Please follow the guide from MXNet which is available at https://mxnet.incubator. apache.org/install/windows_setup.html#install-the-mxnet-package-for-julia .

In short, the user is required to configure MXNet and set an environmental variable before installing the MXNet.jl package.

GitHub repository with source code: https://github.com/PacktPublishing/Hands-On-Computer-Vision-with-Julia/tree/master/Chapter06

Introduction

You may have already seen that running corner detection on a simple image can return thousands of different features, and precisely mapping them with another image could be an issue when using classic computer vision techniques.

We need a tool that can express a human-like behavior to solve this problem quickly and efficiently, and that is where deep learning and neural networks step in.

Deep learning has become one of the hottest topics in the industry. Indeed, neural networks have proven to solve complex problems efficiently, such as image recognition or natural language speech. Luckily for us, we have a solution in Julia to follow the hype!

Let's jump into a quick introduction to neural networks and MXNet and quickly proceed to the programming part.

The need for neural networks

There are millions of use cases requiring that customers build their deep learning application. For a long time, this was a very complicated task involving arcane knowledge and tools which only expert scientists could master.

Remember the process of removing noise from the image by using `erosion`? Depending on complexity, you would be applying it again and again until the image was clean and ready. The neural network could handle this automatically just from training from examples.

Imagine that you have to improve a face-recognition example and match two and tens of other photos from different angles. Your task would be primarily focused on adjusting the threshold and verifying them, again and again, by adjusting the thresholds as you do this.

Today, a simple neural network can replace a computer vision expert in the following areas:

- **Image classification**: This is identifying whether there are cats or dogs in an image
- **Image segmentation**: This is separating an image into multiple segments
- **Image clustering**: This is grouping similar images together
- **Image captioning**: This describes the content of an image in the text
- **Object detection and tracking**: This identifies an object in an image and follows it when it moves

The most amazing thing is that we will cover all of these in this and the subsequent chapter!

The need for MXNet

The benefits of using MXNet over the other packages supporting neural networks such as `KNet.jl`, `Flux.jl`, or `Tensorflow.jl` are the following:

- Requires little experience in both Julia and deep learning
- A large number of pre-trained models and weights
- Has GPU support
- One of the fastest frameworks out there on the market
- Backed by Amazon and Microsoft
- Lastly, it is actively used in production

All of these benefits offer you a privilege so that you can develop a high-performance model in Julia and any time in the process port it to C++, Python, or R and run it in AWS, Azure, or Google.

First steps with the MNIST dataset

MNIST is the dataset that is always discussed first when making first steps in the world of neural networks and image classification. MNIST is a database of grayscale images of handwritten digits. It has a training set of 60,000 examples, and a test set of 10,000 examples.

In the following activities, we will be predicting the value written on an image by building our first neural network.

Getting the data

In order to get to the process of building the neural networks quickly, we will be using the MNIST dataset, which is available in the `MLDatasets.jl` package. The package provides easy and user-friendly access to some of the datasets publicly available out there on the internet. If you don't have the `MLDatasets` package installed, you can do so by running the `Pkg.add` command:

```
Pkg.add("MLDatasets")
```

The moment the MLDatasets package is loaded, the MNIST dataset can be easily downloaded and made available with the `traindata` and `testdata` functions from the MNIST module:

```
using Images, ImageView, MLDatasets
train_x, train_y = MNIST.traindata()
test_x, test_y = MNIST.testdata()
```

The first time you make a call to any of the `MLDatasets` modules, it will present you with **terms of service (TOS)** and offer to download the data to your local machine. Please be aware that depending on a dataset's type, the size can vary and take over 100 MB.

As you can see, both functions return tuples, such as `train_x` and `train_y`. `train_x` corresponds to images of data and `train_y` to the value in an image. The neural network will use the data from `train_x` to train and predict the value of `train_y`.

Next, we will create a preview of a set of the first 10 images from the training dataset. Sometimes, it helps to identify issues with data. This is shown in the following code:

```
preview_img = zeros(size(train_x, 1), 0)

for i = 1:10
  preview_img = hcat(preview_img, train_x[:, :, i])
end

imshow(Gray.(preview_img))
```

We have used `hcat` to join the images together and `imshow` to preview the result:

In order to see what the corresponding values are for each image, we printed out the first 10 values from the `train_y` dataset. This is shown as follows:

```
train_y[1:10]
Main> 5, 0, 4, 1, 9, 2, 1, 3, 1, 4
```

Now that we have seen the data, it is time to move on to creating our first neural network.

Preparing the data

What could be the requirements for our first neural network? It should accept our images as an input, do some magic, and return probabilities for the image corresponding to one of 10 classes—that is, if the number is from 0 to 9.

Unfortunately, MXNet does not accept the images and responses in a format returned by the traindata and testdata functions, and they should both be converted into arrays controlled by MXNet.

From the MNIST dataset, we know that train_x and train_y consist of 60,000 unique images. We will first split the train datasets into two trains and validation into 50,000 and 10,000, accordingly. The validation dataset is required to control the learning process of the neural network and monitor its performance over every round of training:

```
train_length = 50000
validation_length = 10000
```

In the preceding code example, we have defined two variables corresponding to the length of the datasets—train_length and validation_length.

The next step is to convert the train data into a format supported by MXNet. We do this by first predefining the arrays of a type controlled by MXNet, which is shown in the following code:

```
using MXNet

train_data_array = mx.zeros((size(train_x, 1, 2)..., train_length...));
train_label_array = mx.zeros(train_length);

validation_data_array = mx.zeros((size(train_x, 1, 2)...,
validation_length...));
validation_label_array = mx.zeros(validation_length);
```

Next, we copy the data from train_x and train_y to the newly created arrays. As we could see in the preview, our dataset is not ordered, therefore we don't need to shuffle it prior to building our new arrays. This is shown in the following code:

```
for idx = 1:train_length
  train_data_array[idx:idx] = reshape(train_x[:, :, idx],
  (size(train_x, 1, 2)..., 1...))
  train_label_array[idx:idx] = train_y[idx]
end
for idx = 1:validation_length
  validation_data_array[idx:idx] = reshape(train_x[:, :, train_length +
```

```
    idx], (size(train_x, 1, 2)..., 1...))
    validation_label_array[idx:idx] = train_y[train_length + idx]
end
```

The last step is to create an MXNet array data provider; an object connecting data with labels. It also provides an option to set the batch size.

The batch size defines the number of samples that are going to be propagated through the network. Usually, the batch size is set to accept as many samples as can fit into your machine during processing. Because the images in the MNIST dataset are small, we set this to 1,000. In the bigger networks that we will be working with later throughout this book, the batch size might be reduced to as low as 100, 24, 10, or even 1. This is shown in the following code:

```
train_data_provider = mx.ArrayDataProvider(:data => train_data_array,
:label => train_label_array, batch_size = 1000);
validation_data_provider = mx.ArrayDataProvider(:data =>
validation_data_array, :label => validation_label_array, batch_size =
1000);
```

Defining a neural network

So, our data is ready and now it is time to proceed to defining the network itself. To train a model, users are required to perform the following two steps:

1. Configure the model using the `symbol` parameter
2. Then, call `model.Feedforward.create` to create the model

We will start by creating a simple neural network with a hidden layer. MXNet requires us to define the input data, the neural network's structure, and the output layer. We will be using the following three `symbol` parameters to configure the network:

- `mx.Variable` to define the input data
- `mx.FullyConnected` to create a fully connected dense layer
- `mx.SoftmaxOutput` to define the output of the network

Consider the following code to use these:

```
using MXNet

arch = @mx.chain mx.Variable(:data) =>
  mx.FullyConnected(num_hidden=64) =>
  mx.FullyConnected(num_hidden=10) =>
  mx.SoftmaxOutput(mx.Variable(:label))

nnet = mx.FeedForward(arch, context = mx.cpu())
```

The moment you pass the data for the first time, MXNet automatically identifies the input shape of your data and the number of classes for the `SoftmaxOutput` layer.

The `FeedForward` parameter used in the preceding code is used to create the network and configure whether to run it on CPU or GPU. In the case of CPU, the machine will use your computer CPU and RAM to do the analysis and in the case of GPU, it will use your graphics card resources. We will be discussing usage of GPU later in this book.

So, the network is configured and we are left with training and monitoring the performance.

Fitting the network

In order to run the training process, we will call the `mx.fit` function. It provides different sets of parameters and in the following case, we will be using a number of them:

```
mx.fit(nnet, mx.ADAM(), train_data_provider, eval_data =
validation_data_provider, n_epoch = 100, callbacks = [mx.speedometer()]);
```

In the preceding example, we have done the following:

1. `nnet` corresponds to the network we created before.
2. `mx.ADAM` corresponds to a weight `update` function and `ADAM` is proven to converge networks extremely quickly.
3. Next, we pass our train data provider consisting of images and labels.
4. We set the `eval_data` parameter to monitor the performance of our network on `validation_data_provider`.
5. `n_epoch` corresponds to the number of passes over the entire database.
6. `callbacks` is used for additional functions that we would like to evaluate. `mx.speedometer` is providing information on the number of records processed per second.

The results of running the `fit` function are the following:

```
Main>
INFO: Start training on MXNet.mx.Context[CPU0]
INFO: Initializing parameters...
INFO: Creating KVStore...
INFO: TempSpace: Total 3 MB allocated on CPU0
INFO: Start training...
INFO: Speed: 15649.83 samples/sec
INFO: == Epoch 001/100 ==========
INFO: ## Training summary
INFO: accuracy = 0.6949
INFO: time = 3.2204 seconds
INFO: ## Validation summary
INFO: accuracy = 0.8380
INFO: Speed: 49859.40 samples/sec
INFO: == Epoch 002/100 ==========
...
INFO: == Epoch 099/100 ==========
INFO: ## Training summary
INFO: accuracy = 0.9327
INFO: time = 1.0534 seconds
INFO: ## Validation summary
INFO: accuracy = 0.9332
INFO: Speed: 50553.82 samples/sec
INFO: == Epoch 100/100 ==========
INFO: ## Training summary
INFO: accuracy = 0.9327
INFO: time = 0.9950 seconds
INFO: ## Validation summary
INFO: accuracy = 0.9331
INFO: Finish training on MXNet.mx.Context[CPU0]
```

So, in 100 epochs, we have reached 93.3% accuracy. Great results!

Improving the network

But can we do better and go over 93%? Let's add another the `FullyConnected` layer and connect them using activation layers to remove non-linearity to cover the complexity of the task. Consider the following code for it:

```
arch = @mx.chain mx.Variable(:data) =>
  mx.FullyConnected(num_hidden=128) =>
  mx.Activation(act_type=:relu) =>
  mx.FullyConnected(num_hidden=64) =>
```

```
    mx.Activation(act_type=:relu) =>
    mx.FullyConnected(num_hidden=10) =>
    mx.SoftmaxOutput(mx.Variable(:label))

nnet = mx.FeedForward(arch, context = mx.cpu())
mx.fit(nnet, mx.ADAM(), train_data_provider, eval_data =
validation_data_provider, n_epoch = 250, callbacks = [mx.speedometer()]);
```

The preceding model achieves as high as 97.62% accuracy! The output for it is as follows:

```
INFO: == Epoch 155/250 ==========
INFO: ## Training summary
INFO: accuracy = 0.9998
INFO: time = 6.9776 seconds
INFO: ## Validation summary
INFO: accuracy = 0.9762
INFO: Speed: 4499.39 samples/sec
```

Done! With these few lines of code, you have achieved what scientists have been trying to do for years!

Predicting new images

Using the newly trained models on new images requires us to repeat the data preparation step and pass them to the `mx.predict` function. We will try to predict classes for the first `1:10` images from the test dataset. This is done with the following code:

```
data_array = mx.zeros((size(test_x, 1, 2)..., 10));
mx.copy!(data_array, test_x[:, :, 1:10]);

data_provider = mx.ArrayDataProvider(:data => data_array);
results = round(mx.predict(nnet, data_provider; verbosity = 0), 2)

println(results)
```

The `results` variable is a 10x10 matrix where each row represents an image and columns represent the probability for each of the 10 classes. This is depicted with the following output:

```
Main> round.(mx.predict(nnet, data_provider; verbosity = 0), 2)
10×10 Array{Float32,2}:
 0.0 0.0 0.0 1.0 0.0 0.0 0.0 0.0 0.0 0.0
 0.0 0.0 0.99 0.0 0.0 1.0 0.0 0.0 0.0 0.0
 0.0 1.0 0.0 0.0 0.0 0.0 0.0 0.0 0.0 0.0
 0.0 0.0 0.0 0.0 0.0 0.0 0.0 0.08 0.0 0.0
```

```
0.0 0.0 0.0 0.0 0.99 0.0 1.0 0.0 0.0 0.0
0.0 0.0 0.0 0.0 0.0 0.0 0.0 0.0 0.26 0.0
0.0 0.0 0.0 0.0 0.0 0.0 0.0 0.0 0.73 0.0
1.0 0.0 0.0 0.0 0.0 0.0 0.0 0.0 0.0 0.0
0.0 0.0 0.01 0.0 0.0 0.0 0.0 0.0 0.01 0.0
0.0 0.0 0.0 0.0 0.01 0.0 0.0 0.91 0.0 1.0
```

In order to get the actual value, we would use map in combination with findmax to find the class value, which is shown as follows:

```
map(x -> findmax(results[:, x])[2] - 1, 1:10)
```

This would result in the actual value being printed out, such as the one in the following:

```
Main> 7, 2, 1, 0, 4, 1, 4, 9, 6, 9
```

Putting it all together

Let's put all of the preceding code into a single and reusable block. This is shown in the following code:

```
using Images, ImageView, MLDatasets, MXNet

### RETRIEVE DATASET

train_x, train_y = MNIST.traindata()
test_x, test_y = MNIST.testdata()

### SPLIT DATASETS

# creating first neural network
train_length = 50000
validation_length = 10000

train_data_array = mx.zeros((size(train_x, 1, 2)..., train_length...));
train_label_array = mx.zeros(train_length);

validation_data_array = mx.zeros((size(train_x, 1, 2)...,
validation_length...));
validation_label_array = mx.zeros(validation_length);

# The number of records we send to the training should be at least number
of outcome
for idx = 1:train_length
  train_data_array[idx:idx] = reshape(train_x[:, :, idx], (size(train_x, 1,
2)..., 1...))
```

```
    train_label_array[idx:idx] = train_y[idx]
end

for idx = 1:validation_length
  validation_data_array[idx:idx] = reshape(train_x[:, :, train_length +
idx], (size(train_x, 1, 2)..., 1...))
  validation_label_array[idx:idx] = train_y[train_length + idx]
end

### DEFINE NN

arch = @mx.chain mx.Variable(:data) =>
  mx.FullyConnected(num_hidden=128) =>
  mx.Activation(act_type=:relu) =>
  mx.FullyConnected(num_hidden=64) =>
  mx.Activation(act_type=:relu) =>
  mx.SoftmaxOutput(mx.Variable(:label))

nnet = mx.FeedForward(arch, context = mx.cpu())

### CREATE DATA PROVIDER

train_data_provider = mx.ArrayDataProvider(:data => train_data_array,
:label => train_label_array, batch_size = 1000);
validation_data_provider = mx.ArrayDataProvider(:data =>
validation_data_array, :label => validation_label_array, batch_size =
1000);

### TRAIN

mx.fit(nnet, mx.SGD(), train_data_provider, eval_data =
validation_data_provider, n_epoch = 250, callbacks = [mx.speedometer()]);

### PREDICT

data_array = mx.zeros((size(test_x, 1, 2)..., 10));
mx.copy!(data_array, test_x[:, :, 1:10]);

data_provider = mx.ArrayDataProvider(:data => data_array);
results = round(mx.predict(nnet, data_provider; verbosity = 0), 2)

preview_img = zeros(size(test_x, 1), 0)

for i = 1:10
    preview_img = hcat(preview_img, test_x[:, :, i])
end

map(x -> findmax(results[:, x])[2] - 1, 1:10)
```

Done! Feel free to continue your experiments and try achieving higher results!

Multiclass classification with the CIFAR-10 dataset

The CIFAR-10 dataset consists of 60,000 32x32 colorful images in 10 classes, with 6,000 images per class. There are 50,000 training images and 10,000 test images.

Getting and previewing the dataset

Similar to the preceding example, we will use the MLDatasets package to retrieve the CIFAR10 dataset. Let's start by loading the package and having a quick look at the data:

```
using Images, ImageView, MLDatasets, MXNet

train_x, train_y = CIFAR10.traindata()
test_x, test_y = CIFAR10.testdata()
size(train_x)
# Main> (32, 32, 3, 50000)

size(train_y)
# Main> (50000,)

join(unique(train_y), ", ")
# Main> "6, 9, 4, 1, 2, 7, 8, 3, 5, 0"
```

We have used the size function to show the dimensionality of the data and the unique function to list the possible classes. Running the size function on the train_x dataset tells us that we have a training dataset of 500,000 32x32-pixel, 3-channel RGB images. train_y also contains 50,000 images and specifies 10 different classes.

In order to preview the image, we will define an empty three-channel array of a structure identical to the source and combine the first 10 images together. We will also use the `permutedims` function to convert the channel representation to a format supported by Julia. This is shown in the following code:

```
preview_img = zeros((0..., size(train_x, 2, 3)...));

for i = 1:10
 preview_img = vcat(preview_img, train_x[:, :, :, i])
end

imshow(colorview(RGB, permutedims(preview_img, (3, 2, 1))))
```

On a combined image, you will see 32x32-pixel photos of a truck, a car, a horse, a boat, and a cat altogether:

Let's see if we can predict them correctly!

Preparing the data

The moment you get your first look at the data, we will move on to preparing MXNet arrays and creating data providers. The process is very similar to the one we had when working with MNIST except that now we need to handle a dataset of a higher dimensionality. This time, we will also include the creation of a data provider for test images.

Let's start by reserving the memory for our train, validation, and test datasets. We will be creating 4 dimensional MXNet arrays to store the future values:

```
train_length = 40000
validation_length = 10000

train_data_array = mx.zeros((size(train_x, 1, 2, 3)..., train_length...));
train_label_array = mx.zeros(train_length);

validation_data_array = mx.zeros((size(train_x, 1, 2, 3)...,
validation_length...));
validation_label_array = mx.zeros(validation_length);
```

```
test_data_array = mx.zeros((size(train_x, 1, 2, 3)..., size(test_x,
4)...));
test_label_array = mx.zeros(size(test_x, 4));
```

Now, we will iterate over the datasets and populate the arrays:

```
# The number of records we send to the training should be at least number
of outcome
for idx = 1:train_length
    train_data_array[idx:idx] = reshape(train_x[:, :, :, idx],
(size(train_x, 1, 2,3 )..., 1...))
    train_label_array[idx:idx] = train_y[idx]
end

for idx = 1:validation_length
    validation_data_array[idx:idx] = reshape(train_x[:, :, :, train_length
+ idx], (size(train_x, 1, 2, 3)..., 1...))
    validation_label_array[idx:idx] = train_y[train_length + idx]
end

for idx = 1:size(test_x, 4)
    test_data_array[idx:idx] = reshape(test_x[:, :, :, idx], (size(test_x,
1, 2,3 )..., 1...))
    test_label_array[idx:idx] = test_y[idx]
end
```

The moment the datasets are populated, we convert and connect the image data and classes using DataProvider:

```
train_data_provider = mx.ArrayDataProvider(:data => train_data_array,
:label => train_label_array, batch_size = 100, shuffle = true);
validation_data_provider = mx.ArrayDataProvider(:data =>
validation_data_array, :label => validation_label_array, batch_size = 100,
shuffle = true);
test_data_provider = mx.ArrayDataProvider(:data => test_data_array, :label
=> test_label_array, batch_size = 100);
```

We can now move on and proceed with building and testing the neural network.

Starting with the linear classifier

First of all, we will try to create a simple one-layer neural network to set the baseline. We will start with mx.chain and define our network using the Symbolic API. We will use the FullyConnected, Activation, and SoftmaxOutput layers. When the architecture is defined, we will create a model by calling mx.FeedForward. The primary reason for running mx.FeedForward is to set whether the network will run on CPU or GPU:

```
arch = @mx.chain mx.Variable(:data) =>
  mx.FullyConnected(num_hidden=128) =>
  mx.Activation(name=:relu1, act_type=:relu) =>
  mx.FullyConnected(num_hidden=10) =>
  mx.SoftmaxOutput(mx.Variable(:label))

nnet = mx.FeedForward(arch, context = mx.cpu())
mx.fit(nnet, mx.ADAM(), train_data_provider, eval_data =
validation_data_provider, n_epoch = 50, initializer =
mx.XavieInitializer());
```

The performance of the simplest network is way better than random guessing. Considering a quick learning process—not bad at all!

```
INFO: == Epoch 027/050 ==========
INFO: ## Training summary
INFO: accuracy = 0.4810
INFO: time = 0.9088 seconds
INFO: ## Validation summary
INFO: accuracy = 0.4619
```

But this is just the beginning!

Reusing the MNIST architecture

We have already tried running the simplest neural network consisting of a layer and an activation function. Let's see how a more complicated network will perform. We will use the network that has shown a very good performance on the MNIST dataset to see if it performs the same on CIFAR-10. Consider the following code:

```
arch = @mx.chain mx.Variable(:data) =>
  mx.FullyConnected(num_hidden=128) =>
  mx.Activation(act_type=:relu) =>
  mx.FullyConnected(num_hidden=64) =>
  mx.Activation(act_type=:relu) =>
  mx.FullyConnected(num_hidden=10) =>
```

```
   mx.Activation(act_type=:relu) =>
   mx.SoftmaxOutput(mx.Variable(:label))

nnet = mx.FeedForward(arch, context = mx.cpu())
mx.fit(nnet, mx.ADAM(), train_data_provider, eval_data =
validation_data_provider, n_epoch = 100, callbacks = [mx.speedometer()]);
```

Executing the `mx.fit` function will take some time. After 45 epochs, it has an accuracy of around 50% on a validation set. Your expectations were most probably much higher and based a solution that has been working for another example!

```
INFO: == Epoch 45/100 ==========
INFO: ## Training summary
INFO: accuracy = 0.5816
INFO: time = 0.7691 seconds
INFO: ## Validation summary
INFO: accuracy = 0.5081
```

Improving the network

What can be done to improve the network? We can introduce the **convolution neural network (CNN)**. It is a neural network design architecture, which is part of all states of the art solution in image, text, and sound-based classification. The fundamental principle behind CNN is the purpose of convolution, which creates filtered feature maps stacked over each other.

In the following example, every convolution layer will be followed by an activation function to introduce non-linearity:

```
arch = @mx.chain mx.Variable(:data) =>
 mx.Convolution(kernel=(8, 8), num_filter=16, stride = (4, 4)) =>
 mx.Activation(act_type=:relu) =>
 mx.Convolution(kernel=(4, 4), num_filter=32, stride = (2, 2)) =>
 mx.Activation(act_type=:relu) =>
 mx.FullyConnected(num_hidden=256) =>
 mx.Activation(act_type=:relu) =>
 mx.FullyConnected(num_hidden=10) =>
 mx.SoftmaxOutput(mx.Variable(:label))
```

In the preceding example, we have two sets of convolution networks consisting of `mx.Convolution` and `mx.Activation` stacked one under another:

```
INFO: Start training on MXNet.mx.Context[CPU0]
INFO: Initializing parameters...
INFO: Creating KVStore...
```

```
INFO: TempSpace: Total 16 MB allocated on CPU0
INFO: Start training...
INFO: == Epoch 001/250 ==========
INFO: ## Training summary
INFO: accuracy = 0.1297
INFO: time = 9.2072 seconds
INFO: ## Validation summary
INFO: accuracy = 0.1933
....
INFO: == Epoch 026/120 ==========
INFO: ## Training summary
INFO: accuracy = 0.7066
INFO: time = 1.4488 seconds
INFO: ## Validation summary
INFO: accuracy = 0.5704
```

Not bad at all! there is close to a 12% improvement just by introducing the convolution, and the model is still in training!

We can go further and add more complexity to the model. By adding a dropout and pooling layers, we get another few more percent added to the performance when used on a validation set:

```
arch = @mx.chain mx.Variable(:data) =>
        mx.Convolution(kernel=(3, 3), num_filter=32) =>
        mx.Activation(act_type=:relu) =>
        mx.Dropout(p = 0.25) =>
        mx.Pooling( kernel=(2, 2), pool_type=:max) =>
        mx.Flatten() =>
        mx.FullyConnected(num_hidden=256) =>
        mx.Activation(act_type=:relu) =>
        mx.FullyConnected(num_hidden=10) =>
        mx.SoftmaxOutput(mx.Variable(:label))

nnet = mx.FeedForward(arch, context = mx.cpu())
mx.fit(nnet, mx.ADAM(), train_data_provider, eval_data =
test_data_provider, n_epoch = 50, initializer = mx.XavierInitializer());
```

The results will be seen immediately with a much smaller number of epochs:

```
INFO: Start training on MXNet.mx.Context[CPU0]
INFO: Initializing parameters...
INFO: Creating KVStore...
INFO: TempSpace: Total 16 MB allocated on CPU0
INFO: Start training...
INFO: == Epoch 001/250 ==========
INFO: ## Training summary
```

```
INFO: accuracy = 0.1314
INFO: time = 21.4931 seconds
INFO: ## Validation summary
INFO: accuracy = 0.1811
....
INFO: == Epoch 023/150 ==========
INFO: ## Training summary
INFO: accuracy = 0.8454
INFO: time = 5.4200 seconds
INFO: ## Validation summary
INFO: accuracy = 0.6796
```

As you can see, as the network's complexity grows, our results are also improving. Be careful, because the datasets we are using right now are quite large and labeled. Usually, in real-world scenarios, you won't have tens of thousands of images assigned to the correct classes, which makes it very hard to build large networks from scratch.

Let's see what we've got.

Accuracy – why at almost 70

You might be wondering why you can't get the accuracy of your dataset any higher. As there are 10 different classes, pure guessing would give us 10%. Reaching 50% is already a relatively good result. With a number of small improvements, we managed to increase the score and reach 70%, which isn't bad at all. In the following chapters we will cover more techniques to demonstrate how we can go over 80% by using a pretrained set of networks.

Putting it all together

Here, you can find the entire code that has been used in the current chapter:

```
using Images, MLDatasets, MXNet, ImageView

train_x, train_y = CIFAR10.traindata();
test_x, test_y = CIFAR10.testdata();


# preview the images from train_x dataset
preview_img = zeros((0..., size(train_x, 1, 3)...));

for i = 1:10
    preview_img = vcat(preview_img, train_x[:, :, :, i])
end
```

```
imshow(colorview(RGB, permutedims(preview_img, (3, 2, 1))))

### PREPARING THE DATASET

train_x = train_x ./ 1;
test_x = test_x ./ 1;

train_length = 40000
validation_length = 10000

train_data_array = mx.zeros((size(train_x, 1, 2, 3)..., train_length...));
train_label_array = mx.zeros(train_length);

validation_data_array = mx.zeros((size(train_x, 1, 2, 3)...,
validation_length...));
validation_label_array = mx.zeros(validation_length);

test_data_array = mx.zeros((size(train_x, 1, 2, 3)..., size(test_x,
4)...));
test_label_array = mx.zeros(size(test_x, 4));

for idx = 1:train_length
    train_data_array[idx:idx] = reshape(train_x[:, :, :, idx],
(size(train_x, 1, 2,3 )..., 1...))
    train_label_array[idx:idx] = train_y[idx]
end

for idx = 1:validation_length
    validation_data_array[idx:idx] = reshape(train_x[:, :, :, train_length
+ idx], (size(train_x, 1, 2,3 )..., 1...))
    validation_label_array[idx:idx] = train_y[train_length + idx]
end

for idx = 1:size(test_x, 4)
    test_data_array[idx:idx] = reshape(test_x[:, :, :, idx], (size(test_x,
1, 2,3 )..., 1...))
    test_label_array[idx:idx] = test_y[idx]
end

train_data_provider = mx.ArrayDataProvider(:data => train_data_array,
:label => train_label_array, batch_size = 100, shuffle = true);
validation_data_provider = mx.ArrayDataProvider(:data =>
validation_data_array, :label => validation_label_array, batch_size = 100,
shuffle = true);
test_data_provider = mx.ArrayDataProvider(:data => test_data_array, :label
=> test_label_array, batch_size = 100);

### Simple 1-layer NN
```

```
arch = @mx.chain mx.Variable(:data) =>
  mx.Flatten() =>
  mx.FullyConnected(num_hidden=128) =>
  mx.Activation(name=:relu1, act_type=:relu) =>
  mx.FullyConnected(num_hidden=10) =>
  mx.SoftmaxOutput(mx.Variable(:label))

nnet = mx.FeedForward(arch, context = mx.cpu())
mx.fit(nnet, mx.ADAM(), train_data_provider, eval_data =
validation_data_provider, n_epoch = 50, initializer =
mx.XavierInitializer());

### Simple 2-layer NN

arch = @mx.chain mx.Variable(:data) =>
  mx.FullyConnected(num_hidden=128) =>
  mx.Activation(act_type=:relu) =>
  mx.FullyConnected(num_hidden=64) =>
  mx.Activation(act_type=:relu) =>
  mx.FullyConnected(num_hidden=10) =>
  mx.Activation(act_type=:relu) =>
  mx.SoftmaxOutput(mx.Variable(:label))

nnet = mx.FeedForward(arch, context = mx.cpu())
mx.fit(nnet, mx.ADAM(), train_data_provider, eval_data =
validation_data_provider, n_epoch = 50, initializer =
mx.XavierInitializer());

### Convolution Neural Network

arch = @mx.chain mx.Variable(:data) =>
        mx.Convolution(kernel=(3, 3), num_filter=32) =>
        mx.Activation(act_type=:relu) =>
        mx.Dropout(p = 0.25) =>
        mx.Pooling( kernel=(2, 2), pool_type=:max) =>
        mx.Flatten() =>
        mx.FullyConnected(num_hidden=256) =>
        mx.Activation(act_type=:relu) =>
        mx.FullyConnected(num_hidden=10) =>
        mx.SoftmaxOutput(mx.Variable(:label))

nnet = mx.FeedForward(arch, context = mx.cpu())
mx.fit(nnet, mx.ADAM(), train_data_provider, eval_data =
test_data_provider, n_epoch = 50, initializer = mx.XavierInitializer());
```

Good luck trying it out!

Classifying cats versus dogs

The dataset is available on Kaggle (a data science and machine learning competitions platform)—https://www.kaggle.com/c/dogs-vs-cats-redux-kernels-edition. Follow the link to register on the website and download the dataset.

Getting and previewing the dataset

This time, our dataset will consist of a raw images stored on a disk. After downloading the images, I would suggest extracting them to a data folder called Hand-on-Computer-Vision-with-Julia on your machine.

Let's get an understanding of the dataset by loading and previewing some of the images. If you have extracted both archives, your images should be located in the data/train and data/test folders. Every image has a prefix, cat or dog, corresponding to a class followed by a digit corresponding to a sequential number. This is shown in the following code:

```
using Images, ImageView, MXNet

IMAGES_PATH = "data/train"

single_img = joinpath(IMAGES_PATH, "cat.1.jpg")
size(single_img)

imshow(single_img)
```

This will give us a preview image of a cat:

Running the `size` function is showing that the images are very large. The typical size of images that are used in a neural network vary between 96 to 196 in width or height. The code for `size` is as follows:

```
size(single_img)
# Main> (280, 300)
```

Let's run a preview for some more images. We will be resizing the image immediately after loading them so that they fit to the screen:

```
preview_img = zeros(100, 0);

for i = 1:10
    seq_x_img = vcat(
        imresize(load(joinpath($IMAGES_PATH, "cat.$i.jpg")), (50, 50)),
        imresize(load(joinpath($IMAGES_PATH, "dog.$i.jpg")), (50, 50))
    )
    preview_img = hcat(preview_img, seq_x_img)
end

imshow(RGB.(preview_img))
```

From the preview, you can see that the images are very different from each other:

Now that we have an understanding of our dataset, let's proceed to getting it ready for MXNet.

Creating an image data iterator

In the two previous tasks, images were available directly from the `MLDatasets` package. Unfortunately, in real-world scenarios, images are stored on a disk.

Despite the large number of records in the training dataset, we will put them all into memory. To make the process more efficient, we will be resizing the images to 32x32 pixels and converting them to floats. This is shown in the following code:

```
files = readdir(IMAGES_PATH);
data_x = zeros((32, 32, 3, size(files, 1)));
data_y = zeros(size(files, 1));

for idx = 1:size(files, 1)
    file_name = joinpath(IMAGES_PATH, files[idx])

    if endswith(file_name, ".jpg")
        img = imresize(load(file_name), (32, 32))
        data_x[:, :, :, idx] = permuteddimsview(Float16.(channelview(img)),
(2, 3, 1))
        data_y[idx] = 1 * contains(files[idx], "dog")
    end
end
```

The following two class labels are assigned:

- 0 – cat
- 1 – dog

Because of the way we are processing files in the directory, dogs will follow after cats. It makes the dataset ordered and requires shuffling prior to building the data providers. We will be using an 80/20 split. 80% of the data will be used for training and the rest will be used for validation. This is shown in the following code:

```
total_count = size(data_y, 1);
indices = shuffle(1:total_count);
train_indices = indices[1:Int(total_count * 0.8)];
validation_indices = indices[Int(total_count * 0.8) + 1:total_count];
```

Now, we are ready to create the data provider and reference the indices that were defined in the preceding code:

```
train_data_provider = mx.ArrayDataProvider(:data => data_x[:, :, :,
train_indices], :label => data_y[train_indices], batch_size = 100, shuffle
= true);
validation_data_provider = mx.ArrayDataProvider(:data => data_x[:, :, :,
validation_indices], :label => data_y[validation_indices], batch_size =
100, shuffle = true);
```

We are all set for model training!

Training the model

For training the model, we will use the architecture from the CIFAR-10 experiment:

```
arch = @mx.chain mx.Variable(:data) =>
        mx.Convolution(kernel=(3, 3), num_filter=32) =>
        mx.Activation(act_type=:relu) =>
        mx.Dropout(p = 0.25) =>
        mx.Pooling( kernel=(2, 2), pool_type=:max) =>
        mx.Flatten() =>
        mx.FullyConnected(num_hidden=256) =>
        mx.Activation(act_type=:relu) =>
        mx.FullyConnected(num_hidden=10) =>
        mx.SoftmaxOutput(mx.Variable(:label))

nnet = mx.FeedForward(arch, context = mx.cpu())
mx.fit(nnet, mx.ADAM(), train_data_provider, eval_data =
validation_data_provider, n_epoch = 50, initializer =
mx.XavierInitializer());
```

Running the model on CPU can take some time, so please be patient. If you have configured MXNet with GPU support, you are advised to change the `context` to `mx.gpu`.

We have achieved 80% accuracy, which is a good result for such a tiny network:

```
INFO: == Epoch 022/050 ==========
INFO: ## Training summary
INFO: accuracy = 0.9841
INFO: time = 2.4594 seconds
INFO: ## Validation summary
INFO: accuracy = 0.7958
```

Putting it all together

In the following code block, you can find the code that has been used in this section:

```
using Images, MXNet, ImageView

# Loading a single image from the folder
IMAGES_PATH = "data/train"

single_img = load(joinpath(IMAGES_PATH, "cat.1.jpg"))
size(single_img)
imshow(single_img)

preview_img = zeros(100, 0);
```

```
for i = 1:10
    seq_x_img = vcat(
        imresize(load(joinpath(IMAGES_PATH, "cat.$i.jpg")), (50, 50)),
        imresize(load(joinpath(IMAGES_PATH, "dog.$i.jpg")), (50, 50))
    )
    preview_img = hcat(preview_img, seq_x_img)
end

imshow(preview_img)

### PREPARING THE DATASET

files = readdir(IMAGES_PATH);
data_x = zeros((32, 32, 3, size(files, 1)));
data_y = zeros(size(files, 1));

for idx = 1:size(files, 1)
    file_name = joinpath(IMAGES_PATH, files[idx])

    if endswith(file_name, ".jpg")
        img = imresize(load(file_name), (32, 32))
        data_y[idx] = 1 * contains(files[idx], "dog")

        try
            data_x[:, :, :, idx] =
permuteddimsview(Float16.(channelview(img)), (2, 3, 1))
        catch
            data_x[:, :, :, idx] =
permuteddimsview(Float16.(channelview(RGB.(img))), (2, 3, 1))
        end
    end
end

total_count = size(data_y, 1);
indices = shuffle(1:total_count);

total_train_count = Int(total_count * 0.8);
total_validation_count = total_count - total_train_count

train_data_array = mx.zeros((size(data_x, 1, 2, 3)...,
total_train_count...));
train_label_array = mx.zeros(total_train_count);

validation_data_array = mx.zeros((size(data_x, 1, 2, 3)...,
total_validation_count...));
validation_label_array = mx.zeros(total_validation_count);

for idx = 1:total_train_count
```

```
        train_data_array[idx:idx] = reshape(data_x[:, :, :, indices[idx]],
(size(data_x, 1, 2, 3 )..., 1...))
        train_label_array[idx:idx] = data_y[indices[idx]]
end

for idx = 1:total_validation_count
        validation_data_array[idx:idx] = reshape(data_x[:, :, :,
indices[total_train_count + idx]], (size(data_x, 1, 2, 3 )..., 1...))
        validation_label_array[idx:idx] = data_y[indices[total_train_count +
idx]]
end

train_data_provider = mx.ArrayDataProvider(:data => train_data_array,
:label => train_label_array, batch_size = 100, shuffle = true);
validation_data_provider = mx.ArrayDataProvider(:data =>
validation_data_array, :label => validation_label_array, batch_size = 100,
shuffle = true);

arch = @mx.chain mx.Variable(:data) =>
        mx.Convolution(kernel=(3, 3), num_filter=32) =>
        mx.Activation(act_type=:relu) =>
        mx.Dropout(p = 0.25) =>
        mx.Pooling( kernel=(2, 2), pool_type=:max) =>
        mx.Flatten() =>
        mx.FullyConnected(num_hidden=256) =>
        mx.Activation(act_type=:relu) =>
        mx.FullyConnected(num_hidden=10) =>
        mx.SoftmaxOutput(mx.Variable(:label))

nnet = mx.FeedForward(arch, context = mx.cpu())
mx.fit(nnet, mx.ADAM(), train_data_provider, eval_data =
validation_data_provider, n_epoch = 50, initializer =
mx.XavierInitializer());

### Improved neural network

arch = @mx.chain mx.Variable(:data) =>
        mx.Convolution(kernel=(3, 3), num_filter=32) =>
        mx.Activation(act_type=:relu) =>
        mx.Convolution(kernel=(3, 3), num_filter=32) =>
        mx.Activation(act_type=:relu) =>
        mx.Dropout(p = 0.25) =>
        mx.Pooling( kernel=(3, 3), pool_type=:max) =>
        mx.Flatten() =>
        mx.FullyConnected(num_hidden=256) =>
        mx.Activation(act_type=:relu) =>
        mx.FullyConnected(num_hidden=10) =>
        mx.SoftmaxOutput(mx.Variable(:label))
```

```
nnet = mx.FeedForward(arch, context = mx.cpu())
mx.fit(nnet, mx.ADAM(), train_data_provider, eval_data =
validation_data_provider, n_epoch = 50, initializer =
mx.XavierInitializer());
```

Reusing your models

The training of neural networks can be a time-consuming process, so we need to track its progress as the process goes on. We need to learn to save and reload a trained model.

Every MXNet model consist of at least two files:

- `model_name-symbol.json`: Describes the architecture
- `model_name-epoch.params`: Describes the model weights

You can create them yourself or you can download them from the internet. We will cover the process of using pretrained networks in the next chapter.

Saving the model

Saving the model during the training process is done using the `mx.do_checkpoint` callback. A few important parameters are as follows:

- **prefix**: This defines the prefix of the filenames to save the model
- **frequency**: The frequency is measured in epochs to save checkpoints

Let's move back to the MNIST example we have been working on and adjust the `mx.fit` function to include `mx.do_checkpoint`:

```
mx.fit(nnet, mx.ADAM(), train_data_provider, eval_data =
validation_data_provider, n_epoch = 50, callbacks = [mx.speedometer()]);
```

You can see that in the original version we have already configured the network to call the `mx.speedometer` callback. The new version will include a call to `mx.do_checkpoint` to save the model on every 5th epoch with a `weights/mnist` set as a prefix:

```
cp_prefix = "weights/mnist"
callbacks = [
    mx.speedometer(),
    mx.do_checkpoint(cp_prefix, frequency=5)
]
```

```
mx.fit(nnet, mx.ADAM(), train_data_provider, eval_data =
validation_data_provider, n_epoch = 30, callbacks = callbacks);
```

This will also be reflected during the training process:

```
INFO: == Epoch 005/030 ==========
INFO: ## Training summary
INFO: accuracy = 0.9025
INFO: time = 1.9472 seconds
INFO: ## Validation summary
INFO: accuracy = 0.9135
INFO: Saved checkpoint to 'weights/mnist-0005.params'
```

The model architecture will be saved to mnist-symbol.json in the weights folder, while the weights will be saved to mnist-0005.params, mnist-0010.params, and mnist-0015.params, corresponding to the 5th, 10th, and 15th epochs.

Loading the model

Now, we will try to load the saved model and use it to create predictions. MXNet implements the mx.load_checkpoint function, which requires the following set of parameters:

- prefix: This defines the prefix of the file names to save the model
- epoch: Epoch number

Please ensure that you have run the code from the previous activity so that you have all of the required files in place. We will be loading the weights for the 10th epoch:

```
new_nnet = mx.load_checkpoint(cp_prefix, 10, mx.FeedForward);
```

Now, you are ready to create the predictions:

```
data_array = mx.zeros((size(test_x, 1, 2)..., 10));
mx.copy!(data_array, test_x[:, :, 1:10]);
data_provider = mx.ArrayDataProvider(:data => data_array);

results = round.(mx.predict(new_nnet, data_provider; verbosity = 0), 2)
```

The process worked well, with predictions being stored in the results variable.

Summary

In this chapter, you have made your first steps into learning about neural networks and applying them for computer vision tasks. First, we covered the process of image analysis and understanding dimensionality. Next, we learned how to prepare the data so that it can be used with the MXNet deep learning framework. Finally, we built multiple different networks for solving binary and multiclass classification problems.

In the next chapter, we will cover the use of already pretrained models and try to achieve higher scores in the tasks we have accomplished so far.

Questions

Please answer the following questions to confirm what you have learned from the topic:

1. What are the advantages of using neural networks in comparison to classic computer vision?
2. Why do we split the training dataset into training and validation datasets?
3. What are data providers in MXNet and when do you use them?
4. How do you set the size of the input dataset when configuring a neural network architecture?
5. What is `SoftmaxOutput` and why it is used when defining a neural network?
6. How do you define a number for the `SoftmaxOutput` layer?

Further reading

Users are recommend to browse through the Stanford CS231N course on YouTube to understand neural networks in depth.

7
Using Pre-Trained Neural Networks

In this chapter, we will cover the use of pre-trained neural networks from the MXNet Model Zoo and GitHub, compare network performance, and adjust them for solving custom computer vision problems.

The following topics will be covered in this chapter:

- Loading a pre-trained network from the MXNet Model Zoo
- Using Inception V3 and MobileNet v2 classifiers to predict `image` classes
- Using Inception V3 and MobileNet v2 to extract image features
- Using features extracted from Inception V3 to train a new model
- Applying the transfer learning technique and Inception V2 to solve custom problems

Technical requirements

Users are required to have prior knowledge of Julia, but no previous knowledge of math or statistics is required. Minimal experience building neural networks using MXNet is recommended.

Users are required to have `MXNet.jl` installed.

GitHub repository with source code: `https://github.com/PacktPublishing/Hands-On-Computer-Vision-with-Julia/tree/master/Chapter07`

Introduction to pre-trained networks

The usual way of training a neural network consists of the following steps:

1. Preparing and labeling a dataset
2. Developing a neural network architecture
3. Starting to train by initializing weights randomly
4. Training the network and iterating the process once again until the desired result is achieved
5. Saving the model

You would expect to execute the same steps again and again as you start working on a new problem with different data. Instead of training a new network from scratch with randomly initialized weights, you can reuse the structure and weights from another working model which was previously used by you or an open community. The process of using existing neural networks to solve a different problem is referred to as using a pre-trained network. The first network is going to be your pre-trained network. The second one is the network you are going to be fine-tuning.

Transfer learning

There are three typical ways of using pre-trained neural networks. They are listed as follows:

- **Reusing the models**: Consider an example where we apply a pre-trained neural network and retrieve the `image` class. Depending on performance requirements, this could be MobileNet, Inception, VGG, ResNet, or any other that is available out there.
- **Changing the network structure**: Consider an example where we are replacing the last `FullyConnected` and `SoftmaxOutput` layers with a different combination. This would be similar to using a CIFAR-10 model with an MNIST dataset. The difference in the implementation is very tiny and updating the last layers would boost the training time.
- **Feature extraction**: Use a pre-trained network as a feature extractor by using the last layer activations as features. These features can be an input to other neural networks.

Working with a pre-trained network has a number of benefits in comparison to building a new network from scratch, which are enlisted here:

- No need to develop custom architecture
- Very easy to deploy
- Faster training time
- Higher accuracy

First of all, it makes the process of learning much faster and more comfortable than training from scratch. You do not need to work and spend time on deciding the network architecture as the one you will be reusing is already well-tested. Usually, pre-trained networks do not have any special requirements; therefore, it makes the models easy to deploy. Last but not least, there is a higher chance of getting a better score using the pre-trained network as a base.

MXNet Model Zoo

MXNet provides a set of pre-trained neural networks in its Models Zoo. Model `symbol` and `params` files are available at `http://data.dmlc.ml/models/imagenet/`. All models are pre-trained on the ImageNet dataset.

ImageNet is a project which aims to provide image databases for research purposes. It contains more than 14 million images which belong to more than 20,000 classes (or synsets). Most of the pre-trained networks you will ever use will be trained on this dataset.

Predicting image classes using Inception V3

Inception V3 is one of the most widely used neural networks, both as an image classifier and a feature extractor. It has over 75% - 78% accuracy on an ImageNet dataset and is proven to be fast and precise.

Setting up the Inception V3 environment

To start working with Inception V3, you first need to download model files from the MXNet Model Zoo. Use the following links:

- URL: `http://data.dmlc.ml/models/imagenet/`
- ZIP: `inception-v3.tar.gz`

After you have downloaded the archive, please extract it to the `weights/inception-v3` folder.

Loading the network

Loading a pre-trained model is similar to loading your model from a checkpoint. We will use the `mx.load_checkpoint` function to instantiate the model from a checkpoint and also load the `synset` file containing the class names. This is done with the following code:

```
using Images, MXNet

const MODEL_NAME = "weights/inception-v3/Inception-7"
const MODEL_CLASS_NAMES = "weights/inception-v3/synset.txt"

nnet = mx.load_checkpoint(MODEL_NAME, 1, mx.FeedForward);
synset = readlines(MODEL_CLASS_NAMES);
```

The model is loaded and ready to be used for inference!

Preparing the datasets

Every model you use will have some specific requirements for image shape. To use the Inception V3 model, we are required to have `ArrayDataProvider` consisting of normalized three channel images such as `(229, 299, 3)`. Also, as usual, it should be packed to `mx.NDArray`. Consider the following code:

```
img = imresize(load("sample-images/bird-3183441_640.jpg"), (299, 299));
img = permutedims(Float16.(channelview(img)), (3, 2, 1));
```

Next, we will normalize the images:

```
img[:, :, :] *= 256.0;
img[:, :, :] -= 128.;
img[:, :, :] /= 128.;
```

Next, we prepare the MXNet `ArrayDataProvider` consisting of this one image:

```
img = reshape(img, 299, 299, 3, 1);
mx_data = mx.zeros((299, 299, 3, 1));
mx_data[1:1] = img;
data_provider = mx.ArrayDataProvider(:data => mx_data)
```

The dataset is ready to run the predictions!

Running predictions

Running predictions is as simple as calling the `mx.predict` function. Additional work is involved in merging the predictions with `synset`. Refer to the following code:

```
@time pred = mx.predict(mx_model, mx.ArrayDataProvider(:data => mx_data));
# Main> INFO: TempSpace: Total 13 MB allocated on CPU0
# Main> 0.422658 seconds (51.29 k allocations: 5.016 MiB)
```

I have also included the `@time` macro so that we have an approximate time of how long it takes to run the prediction.

Now, it is time to verify the most probable class for our image:

```
mxval, mxindx = findmax(pred[:, 1]);
println(mxval, " ", mxindx, " ", synset[mxindx])
```

We got the following output at `0.48447394 426 n02007558 flamingo`, which means that with 48.5% probability, the most probable class of the image is a flamingo:

You can try changing the path and validating the result on other images.

Expected performance

If you scroll back, you can find that it took nearly half a second to generate the results on the CPU. How good is the speed and should we expect an increase?

According to the MXNet GitHub page, you should get approximately 150 images/second when running on a single K80 GPU. There is not much you can do when running it on a CPU except choose a smaller network, such as MobileNet.

Source: https://github.com/apache/incubator-mxnet/tree/master/example/image-classification

Putting it all together

The entire code for this section is as follows:

```
using Images, MXNet

### LOADING THE MODEL

const MODEL_NAME = "weights/inception-v3/Inception-7"
const MODEL_CLASS_NAMES = "weights/inception-v3/synset.txt"

nnet = mx.load_checkpoint(MODEL_NAME, 1, mx.FeedForward);
synset = readlines(MODEL_CLASS_NAMES);

### PREPARING THE INPUT

img = imresize(load("sample-images/bird-3183441_640.jpg"), (299, 299));
img = permutedims(Float16.(channelview(img)), (3, 2, 1));

img[:, :, :] *= 256.0;
img[:, :, :] -= 128.;
img[:, :, :] /= 128.;

img = reshape(img, 299, 299, 3, 1);

mx_data = mx.zeros((299, 299, 3, 1));
mx_data[1:1] = img;
data_provider = mx.ArrayDataProvider(:data => mx_data);

### PREDICTING

@time pred = mx.predict(nnet, data_provider)
mxval, mxindx = findmax(pred[:, 1]);
println(mxval, " ", mxindx, " ", synset[mxindx])
```

Predicting an image class using MobileNet V2

We have previously discussed how running Inception V3 gives us outstanding results on the ImageNet dataset, but sometimes the inference is considered to be slow. Meet MobiletNet V2, a neural networks architecture developed to deliver excellent results within a short period of time.

Setting up the environment

Unfortunately, MobileNet V2 is not present in the MXNet Model Zoo. We will use two different GitHub repositories to get the `symbol`, `params`, and `synset` files.

Firstly, please navigate to the KeyKy Mobile Net repository (`https://github.com/KeyKy/mobilenet-mxnet`) and download the following two files:

- `mobilenet_v2-0000.params`
- `mobilenet_v2-symbol.json`

Next, navigate to the MobileNet Caffe implementation (`https://github.com/shicai/MobileNet-Caffe`) and download `synset.txt`.

Place all of the downloaded files into the `weights/mobilenet-v2` folder.

Loading the network

You previously loaded Inception V3. The process for this is the same. We will use the `mx.load_checkpoint` function to instantiate the model from a checkpoint and also load the `synset` file containing the class names:

```
using Images, MXNet

const MODEL_NAME = "weights/mobilenet-v2/mobilenet_v2"
const MODEL_CLASS_NAMES = "weights/mobilenet-v2/synset.txt"

nnet = mx.load_checkpoint(MODEL_NAME, 0, mx.FeedForward);
synset = readlines(MODEL_CLASS_NAMES);
```

The model is loaded and ready to be used for inference! Please pay attention to the `load_checkpoint` function. MobileNet loads a checkpoint from epoch 0, instead of 1, which is used for Inception V3.

Preparing the datasets

Preparing datasets for running MobileNet is identical to Inception V3. The only parameter that should be adjusted is the size of the images. MobileNet V2 requires images to be 224 x 244 pixels large. Let's see how we can do this:

1. Let's start by loading the image and converting it to a float and ordering the dimensions as required by MXNet and MobileNet V2:

```
img = imresize(load("sample-images/bird-3183441_640.jpg"), (224,
224));
img = permutedims(Float16.(channelview(img)), (3, 2, 1));
```

2. Next, we normalize the images:

```
img[:, :, :] *= 256.0;
img[:, :, :] -= 128.;
img[:, :, :] /= 128.;
```

3. Next, we prepare the MXNet `ArrayDataProvider` consisting of this one image:

```
img = reshape(img, 224, 224, 3, 1);
mx_data = mx.zeros((224, 224, 3, 1));
mx_data[1:1] = img;
data_provider = mx.ArrayDataProvider(:data => mx_data)
```

The dataset is ready to run the predictions!

Running the predictions

Running a prediction is as simple as calling the `mx.predict` function. The additional work involved is in merging the predictions with `synset`. Consider the following code:

```
@time pred = mx.predict(mx_model, mx.ArrayDataProvider(:data => mx_data));
# Main> INFO: TempSpace: Total 11 MB allocated on CPU0
# Main>  0.198417 seconds (29.07 k allocations: 2.213 MiB)
```

I have also included the `@time` macro so that we have an approximate time for how long it takes to run the prediction. You can see that it is twice as fast as Inception V3. Let's verify whether the prediction is correct:

```
mxval, mxindx = findmax(pred[:, 1]);
println(mxval, " ", mxindx, " ", synset[mxindx])
```

We get the following output at `0.68557036 131 'n02007558 flamingo'`, which is a much better result:

Expected performance

MobileNet V2 is one of the fastest pre-trained classifiers available that has been tested on the ImageNet dataset. You are advised to use this when you are very sensitive to inference time.

Memory requirements are much smaller, which makes it possible to run MobileNet on embedded devices and even Raspberry Pi.

Putting it all together

The entire code for this section is as follows:

```
using Images, MXNet

### LOADING THE MODEL

const MODEL_NAME = "weights/mobilenet-v2/mobilenet_v2"
const MODEL_CLASS_NAMES = "weights/mobilenet-v2/synset.txt"

nnet = mx.load_checkpoint(MODEL_NAME, 0, mx.FeedForward);
synset = readlines(MODEL_CLASS_NAMES);

img = imresize(load("sample-images/bird-3183441_640.jpg"), (224, 224));
img = permutedims(Float16.(channelview(img)), (3, 2, 1));

img[:, :, :] *= 256.0;
img[:, :, :] -= 128.;
img[:, :, :] /= 128.;

img = reshape(img, 224, 224, 3, 1);

mx_data = mx.zeros((224, 224, 3, 1));
mx_data[1:1] = img;
data_provider = mx.ArrayDataProvider(:data => mx_data);

### PREDICTING

@time pred = mx.predict(nnet, data_provider);
mxval, mxindx = findmax(pred[:, 1]);
println(mxval, " ", mxindx, " ", synset[mxindx])
```

Extracting features generated by Inception V3

The first layers of any neural network are basically responsible for identifying low-level features, such as edges, colors, and blobs, but the last layers are usually very specific to the task they are trained for.

Because pre-trained networks are usually trained on a very large dataset such as ImageNet, which contains over 10 million images, it makes those features very generic and possible to be reused for other models.

In the following activity, we will learn how to extract the features from the last activation and use them for solving the CIFAR-10 problem, where we previously achieved around 70% accuracy.

Preparing the network

We assume that you have successfully run the example from the *Predicting an image class using MobileNet v2* section. We will start by loading the network and verifying that the process works, as follows:

```
using Images, MXNet

const MODEL_NAME = "weights/inception-v3/Inception-7"
const MODEL_CLASS_NAMES = "weights/inception-v3/synset.txt"

nnet = mx.load_checkpoint(MODEL_NAME, 1, mx.FeedForward);
synset = readlines(MODEL_CLASS_NAMES);
```

Removing the last Softmax and FullyConnected layers

The process of feature extraction is primarily built on removing the last few layers of the neural network.

Refer to the neural network we developed in the *Introduction to Neural Networks* chapter when trying to solve the MNIST problem:

```
arch = @mx.chain mx.Variable(:data) =>
  mx.FullyConnected(num_hidden=64) =>
  mx.FullyConnected(num_hidden=10) =>
  mx.SoftmaxOutput(mx.Variable(:label))
```

In this network, the `SotmaxOutput` and `FullyConnected` layers with 10 neurons are task-specific. The other `FullyConnected` layer with 64 neurons is the one keeping the features.

In the following activities, we will be removing the `FullyConnected` layers, defining the number of classes, and using the `SoftmaxOutput` layer to define the probabilities and keep the output of a layer we used previously.

In order to remove the last layers from the neural network, it is first important to understand its structure. Let's switch back to Inception V3 and use the `print` function on the `arch` attribute of the `nnet` object to get information about the network's structure:

```
print(nnet.arch)
```

Depending on the size of the network, the output can be large, but we are only focused on the last few layers that should work well. The output is as follows:

```
Op:Flatten, Name=flatten
Inputs:
        arg[0]=global_pool(0)
Variable:fc1_weight
Variable:fc1_bias
--------------------
Op:FullyConnected, Name=fc1
Inputs:
        arg[0]=flatten(0)
        arg[1]=fc1_weight(0) version=0
        arg[2]=fc1_bias(0) version=0
Attrs:
        no_bias=False
        num_hidden=1008
Variable:softmax_label
--------------------
Op:SoftmaxOutput, Name=softmax
Inputs:
        arg[0]=fc1(0)
        arg[1]=softmax_label(0) version=0
Attrs:
        grad_scale=1
        multi_output=False
```

From the preceding output, you can see that the last three layers of our neural network are `Flatten`, `FullyConnected`, and `SoftmaxOutput`. It is also important to remember their names:

- `Flatten` → `flatten`
- `FullyConnected` → `fc1`
- `SoftmaxOutput` → `softmax`

As mentioned earlier, we have no interest in the `FullyConnected` and `SoftmaxOutput` layers, and we want the neural network to return us results that were generated at `flatten`. Each of those layers are represented by a group of additional objects that we will look at now.

Let's get a more detailed view on a network by running the `mx.get_internals` function and saving the name of each layer. As we don't know the real number of layers in a network, we select a relative high number for the `for` loop:

```
layers = mx.get_internals(nnet.arch);
layer_names = Symbol[]

for i = 1:2000
    layer_name = mx.get_name(layers[i])
    push!(layer_names, layer_name)

    if layer_name in [:softmax, :label] break end
end
```

Now, we have saved the names of all the layers in the `layer_names` variable. Let's print the last `10` to see how much it matches what we saw earlier:

```
layer_names[end-9:end]
# Main> 10-element Array{Symbol,1}:
#    :mixed_10_tower_2_conv_batchnorm
#    :mixed_10_tower_2_conv_relu
#    :ch_concat_mixed_10_chconcat
#    :global_pool
#    :flatten
#    :fc1_weight
#    :fc1_bias
#    :fc1
#    :softmax_label
#    :softmax
```

Now, you can see that each layer is represented by more than one object. For example, `SoftmaxOutput` is represented by `:softmax_label` and `:softmax`, but the `FullyConnected` layer is represented by `:fc1_weight`, `:fc1_bias`, and `:fc1`.

In order to create the network that will produce results from the `flatten` layers, we need to remove all layers starting from `:fc1_weight` to `:softmax` and keep the reference to `flatten`:

```
layers_flatten = nothing
layers_to_remove = Symbol[]
```

```
for i = 1:2000
    layer = layers[i];
    layer_name = mx.get_name(layer)
    if layers_flatten == nothing && layer_name == :flatten
        layers_flatten = layer
    elseif layers_flatten != nothing
        push!(layers_to_remove, layer_name)
        if layer_name in [:softmax, :label] break end
    end
end
```

In the preceding code, we do nothing until we reach `flatten`. The moment we find it, we save a reference to `layers_flatten` and add all subsequent names to `layers_to_remove`.

Now, we can proceed with the removal process. We need to update the architecture and remove weights from those layers that we marked for deletion:

```
nnet.arch = layers_flatten

map(x -> delete!(nnet.arg_params, x), layers_to_remove);
map(x -> delete!(nnet.aux_params, x), layers_to_remove);
```

Predicting features of an image

Now, we can try predicting the features of an image. This is done by simply preparing the image in a shape and format required by MXNet and Inception V3 and running the `mx.predict` function. This is shown in the following code:

```
img = imresize(load("sample-images/bird-3183441_640.jpg"), (299, 299));
img = permutedims(Float16.(channelview(img)), (3, 2, 1));

img[:, :, :] *= 256.0;
img[:, :, :] -= 128.;
img[:, :, :] /= 128.;

img = reshape(img, 299, 299, 3, 1);

mx_data = mx.zeros((299, 299, 3, 1));
mx_data[1:1] = img;
data_provider = mx.ArrayDataProvider(:data => mx_data);

@time pred = mx.predict(nnet, data_provider)
```

Done! New features are stored in a `pred` variable. We can use the `size` function to see the dimensionality and the `print` function to print a few columns:

```
size(pred)
# Main> (2048, 1)
print(pred)
# Main> 2048x1 Array{Float32,2}:
#    0.090424
#    0.0208929
#    0.0938953
#    0.144276
#    0.0289061
#    0.258514
   . . .
#    0.478297
#    0.0955287
#    0.132179
#    0.105598
#    0.443035
#    0.21714
#    0.228371
```

So, the size function is showing that we have `2048` values per image and the `print` function is showing that they are of type `float`. So, each and every image we have has been first converted to 299 x 299 x 3 and then to 2,048 features.

Saving the network to disk

We can also save the network to disk under a new name. We will simulate a call to `mx.save_checkpoint`, which is run by the neural network during the training process:

```
mx.save_checkpoint(nnet, "weights/inception-v3/InceptionV3-FE",
mx.OptimizationState(1, 0, 0, 0))
```

Your new network will be located in `weights/inception-v3` and consists of two files:

- `InceptionV3-FE-symbol.json`
- `InceptionV3-FE-0000.params`

You can reuse it anytime by instantiating it from a `0` checkpoint.

Extracting features generated by MobileNet V2

You have already learned how to extract features generated by Inception V3, and now it is time to cover the faster architecture—MobileNet V2.

Preparing the network

Loading MobileNet V2 is in no way different from loading Inception V3. We just need to pay attention to the epoch number when loading the checkpoint. Consider the following code:

```
using Images, MXNet

const MODEL_NAME = "weights/mobilenet-v2/mobilenet_v2"
const MODEL_CLASS_NAMES = "weights/mobilenet-v2/synset.txt"

nnet = mx.load_checkpoint(MODEL_NAME, 0, mx.FeedForward);
```

Removing the last Softmax and FullyConnected layers

We will proceed by looking into the MobileNet V2 structure and understanding which layers we need to keep or remove. We do this by first running the print function on a neural network architecture. This is shown as follows:

```
Op:Pooling, Name=pool6
Inputs:
        arg[0]=relu6_4(0)
Attrs:
        global_pool=True
        kernel=(1, 1)
        pool_type=avg
        pooling_convention=full
Variable:fc7_weight
Variable:fc7_bias
--------------------
Op:Convolution, Name=fc7
Inputs:
        arg[0]=pool6(0)
```

```
            arg[1]=fc7_weight(0) version=0
            arg[2]=fc7_bias(0) version=0
Attrs:
            kernel=(1, 1)
            no_bias=False
            num_filter=1000
            pad=(0, 0)
            stride=(1, 1)
-------------------
Op:Flatten, Name=fc7
Inputs:
            arg[0]=fc7(0)
Variable:prob_label
-------------------
Op:SoftmaxOutput, Name=prob
Inputs:
            arg[0]=fc7(0)
            arg[1]=prob_label(0) version=0
```

In this network, `SoftmaxOutput` and `FullyConnected` `:fc7` will get removed, leaving us with the result of the `Pooling` layer. Let's adjust the code responsible for creating the reference to the `:pool6` and removing the other layers:

```
layers = mx.get_internals(nnet.arch);
layers_flatten = nothing
layers_to_remove = Symbol[]

# We iterate over all layers until we find the one matching our
requirements
# and remove the ones to follow after
for i = 1:2000

    layer = layers[i];
    layer_name = mx.get_name(layer)
    if layers_flatten == nothing && layer_name == :pool6
        layers_flatten = layer
    elseif layers_flatten != nothing
        push!(layers_to_remove, layer_name)
        if layer_name in [:prob] break end
    end
end
```

Because the result is referencing the `Pooling` layer which does not return one-dimensional data, we need to add an additional layer to `Flatten` the data. Flattening a layer is free from any parameters and therefore can be easily added to the model. Consider the following code:

```
nnet.arch = @mx.chain layers_flatten => Flatten()
```

We should also remember to remove the last layers from the network:

```
map(x -> delete!(nnet.arg_params, x), layers_to_remove);
map(x -> delete!(nnet.aux_params, x), layers_to_remove);
```

Now, we are ready to move on to predictions.

Predicting features of an image

We can try predicting the features of an image. This is done by simply preparing the image in a shape and format required by MXNet and Inception V3 and running the `mx.predict` function. This is shown as follows:

```
img = imresize(load("sample-images/bird-3183441_640.jpg"), (224, 224));
img = permutedims(Float16.(channelview(img)), (3, 2, 1));

img[:, :, :] *= 256.0;
img[:, :, :] -= 128.;
img[:, :, :] /= 128.;

img = reshape(img, 224, 224, 3, 1);

mx_data = mx.zeros((224, 224, 3, 1));
mx_data[1:1] = img;
data_provider = mx.ArrayDataProvider(:data => mx_data);

### PREDICTING
@time pred = mx.predict(nnet, data_provider);
```

Done! New features are stored in a `pred` variable. We can use the `size` function to see the dimensionality and the `print` function to print a few columns:

```
size(pred)
# Main> (1280, 1)
```

From what you can see, we have 1,280 features for a single image. This is way less than the number of features generated by Inception V3.

Saving the network to disc

The last step is to save the network using the `mx.save_checkpoint` function:

```
mx.save_checkpoint(nnet, "weights/mobilenet-v2/MobiletNet-FE",
mx.OptimizationState(1, 0, 0, 0))
```

Your new network will be located in `weights/mobilenet-v2` and consists of two files:

- `MobileNet-FE-symbol.json`
- `MobiletNet-FE-0000.params`

You can reuse it anytime by instantiating it from a `0` checkpoint.

Putting it all together

Let's put all the code together and have it available for future chapters:

```
using Images, MXNet

const MODEL_NAME = "weights/mobilenet-v2/mobilenet_v2"
const MODEL_CLASS_NAMES = "weights/mobilenet-v2/synset.txt"

nnet = mx.load_checkpoint(MODEL_NAME, 0, mx.FeedForward);
synset = readlines(MODEL_CLASS_NAMES);

layers = mx.get_internals(nnet.arch);
layers_flatten = nothing
layers_to_remove = Symbol[]

for i = 1:2000

    layer = layers[i];
    layer_name = mx.get_name(layer)
    if layers_flatten == nothing && layer_name == :pool6
        layers_flatten = layer
    elseif layers_flatten != nothing
        push!(layers_to_remove, layer_name)
        if layer_name in [:softmax, :label, :prob] break end
    end
end

nnet.arch = @mx.chain layers_flatten => Flatten()

map(x -> delete!(nnet.arg_params, x), layers_to_remove);
```

```
map(x -> delete!(nnet.aux_params, x), layers_to_remove);

mx.save_checkpoint(nnet, "weights/mobilenet-v2/MobiletNet-FE",
mx.OptimizationState(1, 0, 0, 0))
```

Transfer learning with Inception V3

You have learned to extract features from an image, but now it is important to understand how this can be used to solve custom problems. There are two ways of using the network we created by removing the last layers:

- Use the results that have been generated and pass them to a new network
- Extend the network and add custom `FullyConnected` and `SoftmaxOutput` layers

The two implementations seem to be very similar. So, what are the differences?

- In the first example, you will have two networks—an independent feature extractor and a micro network, which is responsible for classification.
- In the second example, you will have one network doing both tasks. It is also important to note that running a training process may affect the weights of the original network unless they are set to frozen.

In the following example, we will use the Inception V3 feature extractor to train a new model on the Caltech 101 dataset.

Getting the data

Caltech 101 is a dataset of objects belonging to 101 categories. The number of images per category is random and varies from 40 to 800.

In order to download the Caltech dataset, please navigate to `http://www.vision.caltech.edu/Image_Datasets/Caltech101/` and download `101_ObjectCategories.tar.gz` (131 MB).

When the download is complete, please extract it to the `data/101_ObjectCategories` folder.

The dataset was made available by L. Fei-Fei, R. Fergus, and P. Perona, in their book *Learning Generative Visual Models from Few Training Examples: An Incremental Bayesian Approach Tested on 101 Object Categories*. IEEE. CVPR 2004, Workshop on Generative-Model Based Vision. 2004

Preparing the dataset

We will start the process by preparing the dataset. As images are stored in different folders, we need to create a mapping between their path and class.

We do this by iterating over each and every folder and populating a tuple with a location of a photo and ID of the class. The resulting tuple is stored in the `images` array. We also shuffle the `images` array in the end to avoid images being ordered. Consider the following code:

```
using Images, MXNet, StatsBase

DATASET_DIR = "data/101_ObjectCategories"
CLASSES = readdir(DATASET_DIR)

images = Tuple{String,Int}[]

for dir_id = 1:length(CLASSES)

    dir = CLASSES[dir_id]
    all_files = readdir(joinpath(DATASET_DIR, dir))
    keep_files = filter(x -> endswith(x, ".jpg"), all_files)

    append!(images, map(x -> (joinpath(DATASET_DIR, dir, x), dir_id - 1),
keep_files))
end

images = images[shuffle(1:length(images))];
```

Extracting features

Our next step is to extract the features. We will be using the Inception V3 network for this. Because the total number of images is relatively large, I will be using a GPU instance. You can try using a CPU, but it will take a longer to complete.

We will start by instantiating the model in the GPU context:

```
nnet = mx.load_checkpoint("weights/inception-v3/InceptionV3-FE", 0,
mx.FeedForward; context = mx.gpu());
```

We will continue by creating a variable that will store features for the whole dataset. From the previous sections, you should remember that Inception V3 returns 2048 neurons or attributes per image:

```
features = zeros(2048, length(images))
```

Now, we can iterate over images and populate the `features` array. Because running Inception V3 is a memory-consuming task, we will be doing this in batches. Depending on the available memory, please adjust the batch size. For example, running the process on CPU and 8 GB of RAM might require that you decrease the `batch_size_fe` to 50 or 100.

The following process executes the flow:

1. The `for` loop creates an iterator with a step of `batch_size`.
2. `row_count` controls the number of rows, as the last run can have less records than `batch_size`.
3. `mx_data_features` is an MXNet array passed to the model.
4. The second `for` loop executes multiple steps which are combined in one-liners:
    1. Read an image from the disk, resize it to 299 x 299, ensure that the colors are in RGB, and convert it into a three-dimensional representation
    2. Change the order of the dimension to move the channel dimension to the end and reshape it to fit the MXNet array
5. Next, we normalize the dataset as required by the model.
6. Create the data provider, and predict and populate the features array for the records processed in the batch. This is shown in the following code:

```
batch_size_fe = 250
for idx = 1:batch_size:length(images)
    println(idx)

    row_count = min(length(images) + 1 - idx, batch_size_fe)
    mx_data_features = mx.zeros((299, 299, 3, row_count));

    for idx_ = 1:row_count
        img = channelview(RGB.(imresize(load(images[idx + idx_ -
1][1]), (299, 299))))
        mx_data_features[idx_:idx_] =
```

```
    reshape(Float16.(permuteddimsview(img, (3, 2, 1))), (299, 299, 3,
    1));
        end

        mx_data_features *= 256.0;
        mx_data_features -= 128.;
        mx_data_features /= 128.;

        data_provider = mx.ArrayDataProvider(:data =>
    mx_data_features);
        features[:, idx:idx + row_count - 1] = mx.predict(nnet,
    data_provider)
        end
```

Depending on your setup, this process can take some time. I suggest that you use `tmux` if you are running it on a remote Linux machine.

Creating a new network

Our network will be as simple as having input data followed by `FullyConnected` layers and `SoftmaxOutput`. There's no need to add any complexity as the features are already precalculated:

```
arch = @mx.chain mx.Variable(:data) =>
  mx.FullyConnected(num_hidden=length(CLASSES)) =>
  mx.SoftmaxOutput(mx.Variable(:label))

nnet_new = mx.FeedForward(arch, context = mx.gpu())
optimizer = mx.ADAM()
```

Training and validating the results

The next step will be to prepare a training and validation dataset. Our dataset has over 9,000 images and I have made a decision to run the training on the 8000 and leave the rest for validation. I have also defined `batch_size` for training to be as large as the validation dataset. You might need to adjust it to 100, 250, or 500 if you don't have enough resources:

```
train_indices = 1:8000;
valid_indices = 8000:length(images);
batch_size = length(valid_indices);
```

Next, we will create a custom iterator. It will be a `for` loop that will randomly choose images for training and validate them on our validation dataset:

```
for i = 1:30

    println(i, " - ", i+batch_size-1);

    train_indices_batch = sample(train_indices, batch_size, replace =
false);
    valid_indices_batch = sample(valid_indices, batch_size, replace =
false);

    train_data_provider = mx.ArrayDataProvider(:data => features[:,
train_indices_batch], :label => map(x -> x[2],
images[train_indices_batch]), batch_size = batch_size);
    validation_data_provider = mx.ArrayDataProvider(:data => features[:,
valid_indices_batch], :label => map(x -> x[2],
images[valid_indices_batch]), batch_size = batch_size);

    mx.fit(nnet_new, optimizer, train_data_provider, eval_data =
validation_data_provider, n_epoch = 1, callbacks = [mx.speedometer()]);

end
```

We can infer the following from the preceding code—I have used the `sample` function from the `StatsBase` package. It allows me to select indices without replacement. I have referenced both the `features` and `images` datasets. The `features` dataset stores features generated by Inception V3 and the `images` dataset stores the class values.

Depending on your `batch_size`, it can take up to 30 iterations to reach 90%. This 90% is considered to be a very good result. You won't be able to reach it by using the classic computer vision technique:

```
INFO: Start training on MXNet.mx.Context[GPU0]
INFO: Initializing parameters...
INFO: Creating KVStore...
INFO: TempSpace: Total 9 MB allocated on GPU0
INFO: Start training...
INFO: == Epoch 001/001 ==========
INFO: ## Training summary
INFO: accuracy = 0.9144
INFO: time = 0.0041 seconds
INFO: ## Validation summary
INFO: accuracy = 0.9100
INFO: Finish training on MXNet.mx.Context[GPU0]
```

Summary

In this chapter, you learned how to download pre-trained neural networks and use them on custom computer vision problems. You learned to classify images using Inception V3 and MobileNet, analyze network structures, and create feature extractors. Last but not least, you applied the transfer-learning technique and reached 90% on a Caltech 101 dataset.

In the next chapter, we will cover more advanced topics, such as image segmentation and image captioning using neural networks.

Questions

Please answer the following questions:

1. What is the main reason for using pre-trained neural networks?
2. What is the difference between Inception V3 and MobileNet? When would you use one or the other?
3. What are the `symbol` and `params` files of each model?
4. How would you load a pre-trained model from a checkpoint at epoch `10`?
5. How can you adjust a neural network for a custom problem?

Further reading

Users can look into other popular networks such as VGG and ResNet. They are also widely used in the deep learning community.

8
OpenCV

OpenCV is the leading open source library for computer vision, developed over 18 years ago. Since then, it has been made available in any programming language, including Julia. OpenCV is known to be extremely fast, which makes it very effective for executing different processing and for use in real-time applications. We will use the OpenCV and the Julia package and make calls directly to the C++ API.

The following topics will be covered in this chapter:

- Introduction to OpenCV
- Usage of the `OpenCV.jl` package to call basic the `OpenCV` functions
- Usage of the `Cxx.jl` package to call the `OpenCV` function
- Object detection on images using OpenCV
- Object tracking from videos using OpenCV

Technical requirements

Running `OpenCV`, the `OpenCV` package, and the `Cxx` package in Julia has a number of prerequisites. The setup process is very smooth on Linux, has some downsides on macOS, and is close to impossible on Windows machines.

Windows 10 users are suggested for this task to use Julia from a Unix shell or Docker. A detailed step-by-step description on running Ubuntu Linux in Docker on Windows is described at `https://tutorials.ubuntu.com/tutorial/tutorial-windows-ubuntu-hyperv-containers`.

On top of preconfigured operating systems, users are required to have the following setup:

- C++
- OpenCV
- `Images`, `ImageView`, `Cxx`, and `maxruby/OpenCV` packages installed

In order to install `maxruby/OpenCV`, navigate to package GitHub page at `https://github.com/maxruby/OpenCV.jl` and follow the installation instructions to first install Open CV and then the package.

Troubleshooting installation of Open CV

If you experience problems installing Open CV from the source, you can try using the ones installed by `conda` or any other subsystem.

You can read more about Anaconda at their website:

`https://conda.io/docs/user-guide/install/download.html`

In short, the process is as simple as downloading Miniconda or Anaconda from the website, running installation process, and installing Open CV using the `conda install` command:

```
conda install -c conda-forge opencv=3.2.0
```

Troubleshooting installation on macOS

Users might experience problems installing the `Cxx` package and running the `OpenCV` package on macOS. Consider the following code:

```
julia> using OpenCV
INFO: Precompiling module Cxx.
ERROR: LoadError: Failed to precompile Cxx to
/Users/<<username>>/.julia/lib/v0.6/Cxx.ji.
```

There is an issue in GitHub and a number of solutions provided. If you are experiencing a problem running `using Cxx`, complete the following set of steps:

1. Run the following command in the Terminal on macOS `brew install pkg-config` and or use `sudo apt-get install pkg-config` on Linux.
2. When the installation process is complete, start Julia and type `Pkg.dir("Cxx")`.
3. Navigate to the path displayed in the last step. Find the `src` folder and open the `Cxx` package source code folder.
4. Right-click on a `Cxx.jl` and open in an editor such as Sublime, Visual Studio Code.
5. Navigate to line `141` and find the following code—`__precompile__(true)`.

6. Put a hashtag (#) sign in front of the line to comment on it.
7. Get back to Julia and try running `using Cxx` once again.
8. Verify that the package loaded successfully.

With the preceding steps listed, we turn off code precompilation.

Reference: `https://github.com/Keno/Cxx.jl/issues/369`

First steps with OpenCV

In the previous chapters, we have covered different Julia packages dedicated to image processing and used MXNet to develop and create neural networks.

Now we take a step aside and try using a different image processing solution available in Julia—OpenCV. OpenCV is a set of highly optimized functions that can be used simply in data and image preparation tasks, performing adjustment, and enhancement tasks, and for tasks such as face recognition, object detection, camera, and object movements.

We start by performing simple steps, such as image loading and executing examples, and proceed to neural network module. Be aware that because the `OpenCV.jl` package implements only a small fraction of Open CV functionality, you will primarily code in C++ and only expose the final results to Julia.

Updating OpenCV package source code

In order to get Open CV modules used in this chapter, we need to modify the source code of the package and add those that are missing:

1. Start Julia and type `Pkg.dir("OpenCV")`.
2. Navigate to the path displayed in the last step. Find the `src` folder to open the `OpenCV` package source code folder.
3. Right-click on `OpenCV_libs.jl` and open in an editor such as Sublime, Visual Studio Code.
4. On lines `12-29`, you should find a list of modules the package will be loading from Open CV.
5. Update the list to include `dnn` after `imgproc`.

Look at the following example on how the list should look:

```
libNames = [
  "shape",
  "stitching",
  "objdetect",
  "superres",
  "videostab",
  "calib3d",
  "features2d",
  "highgui",
  "videoio",
  "imgcodecs",
  "video",
  "photo",
  "ml",
  "imgproc",
  "dnn",
  #"flann", // TODO: resolve typeid error due to rtti flag
  "viz"
]
```

6. Also, adjust the `version` number according to the OpenCV version installed on your machine.
7. Save the file and restart Julia.

Defining Open CV location

In order to be able to successfully run Open CV I help `Pkg Config` to find the Open CV, search for `opencv.pc` on your machine to find its location. Use the path to set `PKG_CONFIG_PATH` when in Julia:

```
ENV["PKG_CONFIG_PATH"] = "/path/to/pkgconfig-folder"
```

I will be using the following example throughout the book, that is, the location of the file on my machine:

```
ENV["PKG_CONFIG_PATH"] = "/Users/dc/anaconda/envs/python35/lib/pkgconfig"
```

Testing whether OpenCV works

First, let's try running the code to confirm that your setup works:

```
range = cvRange(1,100)

# Main> (class cv::Range) {
#  .start = (int &) 1
#  .end = (int &) 100
#}
```

If the code runs successfully and the output matches, you are well set and ready to proceed further.

Working with images

Working with images coming from OpenCV is slightly different from working with images in the `Images.jl` package.

Converting OpenCV Mat to Julia images

Julia images are different from Open CV images, and that is because Open CV is run by C++ in the backend. Therefore, we need a way to convert an image prepared in Open CV `Mat` to Julia format.

The `OpenCV.jl` package does not have any functions to accomplish the task, and therefore I have created one. It is not the fastest function ever, but it can work well when run multiple times:

```
using Images
using OpenCV
using Cxx

function opencv_to_image(img_opencv)

converted_image = zeros(Float16, (3, rows(img_opencv), cols(img_opencv)));

    for i = 1:size(converted_image, 2)
        for j = 1:size(converted_image, 3)
            pixel_value = @cxx at_v3b(img_opencv, i, j)
            converted_image[:, i, j] = map(x -> Float16(at(pixel_value,
            x)), [2, 1, 0]) ./ 255.0
        end
```

```
        end

    return converted_image
end
```

Reading images

The first and basic operation we will cover is reading and writing the images returned by Open CV functions.

Note that in order to load or save the image, you need to provide a full path to the file.

We start the example with introducing the location to OpenCV library and proceed with the `imread` function, which is part of the `OpenCV` package:

```
filename = joinpath(pwd(), "sample-images", "cat-3352842_640.jpg");
img = imread(filename);
```

After a successful run, you will have the `img` variable consisting of the `OpenCV` `Mat` image. It is no Julia image that you have worked with, and any of the transformations you have learned won't work.

 Be aware of the semicolon at the end of the `imread` function. It is very important to put it after every function that calls the `OpenCV` or `Cxx` function. The reason is that Julia might not know how to output the results to the interface and fail with an exception.

Saving images

Saving images is very simple. It is only important to specify the full path. As in the preceding example, we will use `pwd()` to reference current directory:

```
imwrite(joinpath(pwd(), "cat-copy.png"), img)
```

Destroying the object

In order to avoid problems with memory allocation when using C++, it is recommended that you release C++ objects when you are done working with them.

Consider the following example:

```
filename = joinpath(pwd(), "sample-images", "cat-3352842_640.jpg");
img = imread(filename);
```

The `img` object contains a reference to a C++ object. Setting `img` to nothing does not guarantee that C++ resources will be released until you close Julia.

In order to release the resource, you need to call the `destroy` function, which is part of the `Open CV` package:

```
destroy(img)
```

Image capturing from web camera

We are starting our introduction to advanced image processing with capturing the content from a video camera.

Capturing frame from the camera is be done in multiple steps:

1. Identifying the camera
2. Capturing the frame
3. Converting the frame to Julia images
4. Previewing the result

We will also find the most efficient way of getting the results to Julia images; that is, running the conversion process from C++ on a Julia side or saving and reloading the image.

First, we start by initializing libraries and configuration parameters:

```
ENV["PKG_CONFIG_PATH"] = "/Users/dc/anaconda/envs/python35/lib/pkgconfig"

using OpenCV
using Images
using Cxx
```

Next, we proceed with defining the function to convert Open CV images to Julia images:

```
function opencv_to_image(img_opencv)

    converted_image = zeros(Float16, (3, rows(img_opencv),
    cols(img_opencv)));

    for i = 1:size(converted_image, 2)
```

```
        for j = 1:size(converted_image, 3)
            pixel_value = @cxx at_v3b(img_opencv, i, j)
            converted_image[:, i, j] = map(x -> Int(at(pixel_value,
            x)), [2, 1, 0]) ./ 255
        end
    end

    return converted_image
end
```

Julia code is ready, and we need to proceed with defining C++ code. C++ code is defined within the cxx""" <<C++ code>> """ tag. As the code is put inside """, we should first come up with all code and then execute it in REPL.

We start with initializing C++ libraries and namespaces. Next, we define the first function that will connect to the web camera. Connection to the web camera is done by initializing the VideoCapture class from Open CV namespace and reading the first frame:

```
#include "opencv2/videoio.hpp"
#include "opencv2/imgproc.hpp"

using namespace std;
using namespace cv;

/// Retrieve video device by index
cv::VideoCapture get_video_device(int device_index) {

    cv::VideoCapture capture(device_index);
    cv::Mat frame;

    capture.read(frame);

    return capture;
}
```

When we know how to connect to the web camera, we need to define a function to capture and return the frame. It is done by calling the read function of the VideoCapture object. This is shown in the following code:

```
/// Capture frame
cv::Mat capture_frame(cv::VideoCapture capture) {
    cv::Mat frame;
    bool Success = capture.read(frame);
    return frame;
}
```

We also add another function that will capture the frame, but instead of returning it to Julia, we save the image to disk. The implementation is very similar to `capture_frame`, but we also use the `success` status and the `imwrite` function to save the file:

```
/// Capture and save frame
void capture_save_frame(cv::VideoCapture capture, String dest) {
    cv::Mat frame;
    bool success = capture.read(frame);

    if (success) {
        cv::imwrite(dest, frame);
    }
}
```

The last C++ function we define is responsible for releasing the camera resources:

```
/// Release an active camera
void release_camera(cv::VideoCapture capture) {
    capture.release();
}
```

Now, let's proceed to calling the the functions and getting the results. We start with creating a `video_device` object keeping a reference to our web camera. CAP_ANY determines the camera; in this case, it is equal to zero and returns a built-in web camera:

```
video_device = @cxx get_video_device(CAP_ANY);
```

Next, we test two different scenarios. First, we try to read the frame and convert the OpenCV `Mat` object to a Julia image. We also use the `@time` macro to have a rough estimate of the execution time:

```
@time current_frame = @cxx capture_frame(video_device);
# Main> 0.011622 seconds (7 allocations: 400 bytes)

@time current_frame_image = opencv_to_image(current_frame);
# Main> 6.573967 seconds (9.12 M allocations: 439.680 MiB, 2.15% gc time)

imshow(colorview(RGB, current_frame_image));
```

You can see that the code is very inefficient. Let's try running `capture_save_frame` and reloading the image from Julia:

```
filename = joinpath(pwd(), "camera-frame.jpg");

@time @cxx capture_save_frame(video_device, pointer(filename));
# Main> 0.080999 seconds (7 allocations: 304 bytes)

@time current_frame_image_2 = load(filename);
# Main> 0.034937 seconds (265 allocations: 7.046 MiB)

imshow(current_frame_image_2)
```

This option is way better. It does not allocate that much memory and is over 50 times better. I suspect that the timing can be decreased by resizing the image when it is captured and operating with a smaller resolution.

Both results will output a photoshoot from your web camera. You can see the view from my place in the following photo:

As the code contains a mix of C++ and Julia code, I urge you to review the GitHub version to ensure that you implement it correctly.

Face detection using Open CV

Now that you have learned to get the content from a camera, we can proceed with extending the C++ code and adding the face detection functionality. We will learn how to draw the bounding boxes, get the coordinates, and crop the face:

We start by initializing the Julia packages:

```
ENV["PKG_CONFIG_PATH"] = "/Users/dc/anaconda/envs/python35/lib/pkgconfig"

using OpenCV
using Images, ImageView
using Cxx
```

The moment packages are loaded, we proceed to defining C++ code. C++ code is defined within the cxx""" <<C++ code>> """ tag and then executed in REPL.

The first thing to do in the C++ code is defining and including the libraries. We include both standard C++ and Open CV libraries:

```
#include "opencv2/objdetect.hpp"
#include "opencv2/highgui.hpp"
#include "opencv2/imgproc.hpp"

#include <iostream>
#include <stdio.h>

using namespace std;
using namespace cv;
```

Now, we are ready to proceed with developing the functions. Open CV supports different types of classifiers to detect an object. We will be using the `Haar` classifier and preloading its definition from `.xml`. It will be responsible for finding faces on a photo. Consider the following code:

```
/// Load cascade file
CascadeClassifier load_face_cascade(String face_cascade_name) {

    CascadeClassifier face_cascade;
    face_cascade.load(face_cascade_name);

    return face_cascade;
}
```

Next, we proceed with defining a function that will execute the classifier and draw a bounding box around the face. In order to achieve the goals, we will first convert the image to grayscale, equalize its histogram, and run the cascade classifier to detect the faces.

The moment faces are found, we will draw bounding boxes around each of them. This function is capable of finding multiple faces:

```
/// detect and draw a bounding box on the image
void detect_face(cv::Mat frame, CascadeClassifier face_cascade) {
    std::vector<Rect> faces;
    cv::Mat frame_gray;

    cvtColor( frame, frame_gray, COLOR_BGR2GRAY );
    equalizeHist( frame_gray, frame_gray );

    face_cascade.detectMultiScale( frame_gray, faces, 1.1, 2,
     0|CASCADE_SCALE_IMAGE, Size(30, 30) );

    for( size_t i = 0; i < faces.size(); i++ ) {
        Point center( faces[i].x + faces[i].width/2, faces[i].y +
        faces[i].height/2 );
        ellipse( frame, center, Size( faces[i].width/2,
        faces[i].height/2), 0, 0, 360, Scalar( 255, 0, 255 ),
        4, 8, 0 );
    }
}
```

The other function we will develop is responsible for returning the actual coordinates of a bounding box. It accepts an image and `cascade` classifier as an input and does a job similar to the function drawing the bounding boxes, but instead of drawing the boxes, it returns values for the x and y axes, and width and height.

You can try extending the function to accept `face_id` as a parameter, because, for now, it will only return coordinates for the first face:

```
/// detect and return bounding box coordinates
std::vector<int> detect_face_coords(cv::Mat frame, CascadeClassifier
face_cascade) {
    std::vector<Rect> faces;
    cv::Mat frame_gray;
    std::vector<int>vec(4);

    cvtColor( frame, frame_gray, COLOR_BGR2GRAY );
    equalizeHist( frame_gray, frame_gray );

    face_cascade.detectMultiScale( frame_gray, faces, 1.1, 2,
     0|CASCADE_SCALE_IMAGE, Size(30, 30) );

    if (faces.size() > 0) {
        vec[0] = faces[0].x;
        vec[1] = faces[0].width;
        vec[2] = faces[0].y;
        vec[3] = faces[0].height;
    }
    else {
        vec[0] = 0; vec[1] = 0;
        vec[2] = 0; vec[3] = 0;
    }
    return vec;
}
```

We are done defining C++ code and are ready to proceed to Julia with pure Julia syntax. First, we download the `cascade` classifier from Open CV GitHub page and pass it to the `load_face_cascaade` function:

```
cascade_path =
download("https://raw.githubusercontent.com/opencv/opencv/master/data/haarc
ascades/haarcascade_frontalface_alt.xml")
face_cascade = @cxx load_face_cascade(pointer(cascade_path));
```

Next, we will try different scenarios:

- Draw the bounding boxes around image and save it to disk
- Retrieve the bounding box coordinates and crop the image to only keep the face

Drawing bounding boxes and saving the image to disk is fairly simple. We will use the `imread` function from Open CV package to read the image from disk and pass it to the `detect_face` function; `detect_function` does not return any results and modifies an existing object in `img_opencv`. Next, we will save the image to disk using the `imwrite` function from Open CV package, as follows:

```
filename = joinpath(pwd(), "sample-images",
"beautiful-1274051_640_100_1.jpg");
img_opencv = imread(filename);
@cxx detect_face(img_opencv, face_cascade);
imwrite(joinpath(pwd(), "detect-faces.jpg"), img_opencv)
```

You should find the result in your project folder under `detect-faces.jpg`:

In the second example, we are retrieving actual bounding boxes and cropping the image. We will not overcomplicate the task and preload image in both Open CV and Julia formats, and we will use Open CV image to identify the coordinates and apply them to Julia image:

```
filename = joinpath(pwd(), "sample-images",
"beautiful-1274051_640_100_1.jpg");
img_opencv = imread(filename);
img_images = load(filename);

coords_cxx = @cxx detect_face_coords(img_opencv, face_cascade);
coords = map(x -> Int(at(coords, x)), 0:3);

face = img_images[coords[3]:coords[3] + coords[4], coords[1]:coords[1] +
coords[2]]
imshow(face)
```

In the preceding example, we used the `map` function to iterate over the array returned by Open CV and create an area of interest. All this results in the face being cropped very precisely:

Done! Now you know how to identify people in an image. As for the previous example, I encourage you to browse through the GitHub code.

Object detection using MobileNet-SSD

We will be using MobileNet-SSD network to detect objects such as cats, dogs, and cars in a photo. A combination of MobileNet and SSD gives outstanding results in terms of accuracy and speed in object detection activities. At the end of the section, you will be able to generate images containing bounding box and name of the object:

We always start the same, by loading Julia packages and defining path to `opencv.pc`:

```
ENV["PKG_CONFIG_PATH"] = "/Users/dc/anaconda/envs/python35/lib/pkgconfig"

using OpenCV
using Images, ImageView
using Cxx
```

The moment Julia packages are defined, we proceed to writing C++ code. Remember that C++ code is encapsulated within special syntax, as follows:

```
cxx"""
  <<C++ code goes here>>
"""
```

The first thing when starting to write code in C++ is to add all prerequisites, and we will have a number of them in the example:

```
#include <opencv2/dnn.hpp>
#include <opencv2/imgproc.hpp>
#include <opencv2/highgui.hpp>

#include <fstream>
#include <iostream>
#include <cstdlib>

using namespace std;
using namespace cv;
using namespace cv::dnn;
```

Next, we will define a function to initialize our neural network. It will accept path for prototxt and caffemodel and preload the model to memory using the readNetFromCaffe function:

```
Net load_model(String caffe_model_txt, String caffe_model_bin) {

    Net net = dnn::readNetFromCaffe(caffe_model_txt, caffe_model_bin);

    if (net.empty()) {
        std::cerr << "Can't load network." << std::endl;
        exit(-1);
    }

    return net;
}
```

Next, we will proceed to the main program logic, that is, running neural network and processing the results.

We will execute the following set of actions:

1. Accept image and neural network as input parameters.
2. Define possible outcomes/classes.
3. Prepare image for classification. MobileNet-SSD requires images to be 300x300 pixels large.
4. Run the neural network and collect the results.
5. Go over the results and remove the ones that have a confidence lower than a specific threshold.
6. Draw bounding boxes around confident results.

This is shown with the following code:

```
void detect_objects(Mat img, Net net) {

 string CLASS_NAMES[] = {"background", "aeroplane", "bicycle", "bird",
"boat", "bottle", "bus", "car", "cat", "chair", "cow", "diningtable",
"dog", "horse", "motorbike", "person", "pottedplant", "sheep", "sofa",
"train", "tvmonitor"};

    // prepare image for evaluation
    Mat scaled_image;
    resize(img, scaled_image, Size(300,300));
    scaled_image = blobFromImage(scaled_image, 0.007843, Size(300,300),
     Scalar(127.5, 127.5, 127.5), false);

    // run the network
    net.setInput(scaled_image, "data");
    Mat detection_out = net.forward("detection_out");
    Mat results(detection_out.size[2], detection_out.size[3], CV_32F,
    detection_out.ptr<float>());
    // draw bounding boxes if the probability is over a specific
    threshold
    float threshold = 0.5;
    for (int i = 0; i < results.rows; i++) {

        float prob = results.at<float>(i, 2);

        if (prob > threshold) {
            int class_idx = static_cast<int>(results.at<float>(i, 1));
            int xLeftBottom = static_cast<int>(results.at<float>(i, 3)
            * img.cols);
            int yLeftBottom = static_cast<int>(results.at<float>(i, 4)
            * img.rows);
            int xRightTop = static_cast<int>(results.at<float>(i, 5) *
```

```
        img.cols);
        int yRightTop = static_cast<int>(results.at<float>(i, 6) *
        img.rows);

        String label = CLASS_NAMES[class_idx] + ": " +
        std::to_string(prob);

        Rect bounding_box((int)xLeftBottom, (int)yLeftBottom, (int)
        (xRightTop - xLeftBottom), (int)(yRightTop - yLeftBottom));
        rectangle(img, bounding_box, Scalar(0, 255, 0), 2);
        putText(img, label, Point(xLeftBottom, yLeftBottom),
        FONT_HERSHEY_SIMPLEX, 0.5, Scalar(0,0,0));
    }
  }
}
```

Now when the C++ code is ready, we are ready to switch to Julia code. We start by downloading models weights as described in the documentation. Normally, these weights are located in the official GitHub repository at `https://github.com/chuanqi305/MobileNet-SSD`.

Consider the following code:

```
# source:
https://github.com/opencv/opencv_extra/blob/master/testdata/dnn/download_models.py

caffemodel_path = joinpath("data", "MobileNetSSD_deploy.caffemodel")
if ~isfile(caffemodel_path)
download("https://drive.google.com/uc?export=download&id=0B3gersZ2cHIxRm5PMWRoTkdHdHc", caffemodel_path) end

prototxt_path = joinpath("data", "MobileNetSSD_deploy.prototxt")
if ~isfile(prototxt_path)
download("https://raw.githubusercontent.com/chuanqi305/MobileNet-SSD/master/MobileNetSSD_deploy.prototxt", prototxt_path) end
```

It can take some time to download the models. We will download them once and store them in the `data` folder.

The moment weights are ready, we are good to go and initialize our neural network:

```
opencv_dnn_model = @cxx load_model(pointer(prototxt_path),
pointer(caffemodel_path));
```

Now, we can start testing the models in different scenarios. Let's cover some of them in the following sections.

We will repeat the same actions for different images. We read the image to Open CV format using the imread function. We call detect_objects to draw the bounding boxes and save the result using the imwrite function:

```
filename = joinpath(pwd(), "sample-images", "cat-3352842_640.jpg");
img_opencv = imread(filename);
@cxx detect_objects(img_opencv, opencv_dnn_model);
imwrite(joinpath(pwd(), "object-detection-1.jpg"), img_opencv)

filename = joinpath(pwd(), "sample-images", "bird-3183441_640.jpg");
img_opencv = imread(filename);
@cxx detect_objects(img_opencv, opencv_dnn_model);
imwrite(joinpath(pwd(), "object-detection-2.jpg"), img_opencv)

filename = joinpath(pwd(), "sample-images", "kittens-555822_640.jpg");
img_opencv = imread(filename);
@cxx detect_objects(img_opencv, opencv_dnn_model);
imwrite(joinpath(pwd(), "object-detection-3.jpg"), img_opencv)
```

You should have three new images in the root folder, each corresponding to one of the images we analyzed. You can see that despite of the different content and number of objects, the network worked very well:

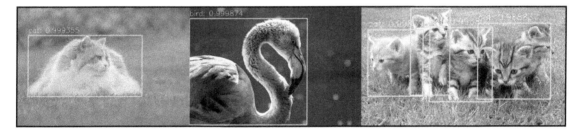

It is possible to retrain the model using custom dataset and number of classes. Refer to the Mobilenet-SSD page for more details:

https://github.com/chuanqi305/MobileNet-SSD

Summary

In this chapter, you learned the basic C++ syntax and used it from Julia to call Open CV functions. You tried using different Open CV modules for loading video stream, processing images, and running pretrained neural networks.

By the end of the chapter, you had learned how to do a face and object detection on an image.

Questions

Answer the following questions:

1. How do you define C++ code in Julia?
2. How do you call C++ functions in Julia?
3. When and why do you need to destroy objects coming from Open CV?
4. What was the most efficient way we found for getting Open CV images to Julia?
5. What type of classifier have we used to run face detection?
6. What was the number of classes we predict in the *Object detection using MobileNet-SSD* section?

Assessments

Chapter 1

1. Which package(s) are required to load an image from a disk?

   In order to load an image you are required to have `Images.jl` package.

2. Which package is required to download a file from the internet?

   No packages are required. `download` function is part of Julia Base package.

3. Which types of files/file extensions are returned by the `readdir` function?

   `readdir` returns all files in a folder.

4. Which function is used to save an image to disk? What are the prerequisites for saving a file to disk?

   `save` function is used to save file to disk. It accepts 2 parameters - destination path with file name in one of the image formats, such as `png` or `jpg` and image in Julia Images file. Destination path (folder) should exist on disk.

5. What is the most noticeable difference when saving images in JPG or PNG formats?

   There are few noticeable difference - first PNG can keep the transparency and has better quality.

6. What is the difference between scale and resize?

   Resizing images does not keep the image proportions compared to scaling.

Chapter 2

1. What is the difference between `Gray` and `RGB` image representation?

   `Gray` images are represented in 1 channel compared to `RGB` which are represented in 3 channels.

2. When would you use the `channelview` function?

   `channelview` function is used to decompose or split out the color channels to a separate dimensions.

3. When would you use the `permuteddimsview` function?
   `permuteddimsview` function is used change the order of channels in an image.

4. What is the difference between using the Fill function and one of the border padding effects?
   `Fill` function is used to fill the border with a constant value, compared to border padding that duplicates the content of an image.

5. How did we achieve the image sharpening effect?
   We created a sharpened version of an image by subtracting Gaussian smoothed image from the original version.

Chapter 3

1. What is a structuring element in the `ImageMorphology` package?

   The structuring element is usually a 3x3 binary block that slides over the image and updates it.

2. When would you use the `channelview` function?

   It is a block of 3x3 pixels.

3. What are the prerequisites for the image color scheme before applying morphological processing?
   Images should be in binary or grayscale.

4. What is the difference between the `erode` and the `dilate` functions?
   Erode shrinks the image's foreground or 1-valued objects, compared to dilate which does the opposite and grows it.

5. What is the difference between the `erode` and the `opening` functions?
   Opening compared to erode tries to keep large objects untouched and remove small noise.

6. When would you use a combination of the `tophat` and `bothat` functions?
   Combination of `tophat` and `bothat` is used to improve contrast of an image.

Chapter 4

1. What is the primary difference between seeded regions growing and the fast scanning algorithm?

   Seeded region growing algorithm requires us to supply the coordinates of the object, compared to fast scanning which does it automatically.

2. When would you use supervised image segmentation algorithms, such as the seeded region growing technique?

   I would you seeded region growing when manually annotating images for deep learning activities.

3. How does increasing and decreasing the threshold merging step parameter for the Felzenszwalb algorithm affect the results?
   Increasing the threshold merging step decreases number of segments.

4. When would you use the segment pruning technique?
   I would use segment pruning technique to remove noisy "segments" that are taking a really small area.

Chapter 5

1. What is the purpose of corner detection?

   Corner detection is widely used for feature extraction from an image.

2. How can corner detection help to identify areas with text?

   Areas having a text will have a high intensity of corners.

3. How does the increase of the threshold value for FAST affect the number of features?

   Increasing threshold value decreases number of features returned by FAST.

4. When would you use a BRIEF algorithm, and when would you use a BRISK one?

   I would use BRIEF when I exactly knew that images are not scaled and rotated. That would give a slight boost comparing to BRISK.

5. What is the primary difference between an ORB algorithm and BRISK?

   Main difference between ORB and BRISK is that BRIS is scale invariant.

6. Which of the three algorithms (BRIEF, ORB, and BRISK) implements FAST out of the box?

   ORB runs FAST out of the box and therefore it requires less adjusting.

Chapter 6

1. What are the advantages of using neural networks in comparison to classic computer vision?

   Neural network can learn complicated relationships between image shapes compared to classic Open CV approach when you open.
2. Why do we split the training dataset into training and validation datasets?

   It is done in order not to over fit during the training process.
3. What are data providers in `MXNet` and when do you use them?

   We have extensively used `ArrayDataProvider` that we have filled with different value. It is also possible to use `ImageDataProvider` but it has some prerequisites to the format.
4. How do you set the size of the input dataset when configuring a neural network architecture?

   It is identified automatically the moment you pass the first dataset.
5. What is `SoftmaxOutput` and why it is used when defining a neural network?

   `SoftmaxOutput` defines an output of the network. Each predicted class will get it
6. How do you define a number for the `SoftmaxOutput` layer?

   Number of outcomes in `SoftmaxOutput` layers is defined using last `FullyConnected` layer.

Chapter 7

1. What is the main reason for using pre-trained neural networks?

   The main reason of using pre-trained neural networks is that they make the training process much faster and more comfortable.

2. What is the difference between Inception V3 and MobileNet? When would you use one or the other?
Inception V3 is slower to run but has higher accuracy. MobileNetV2 is extremely fast but less precise than Inception V3. I would use Inception V3 when running batch jobs and MobileNet V2 for real-time applications.

3. What are the symbol and params files of each model?

   `symbol` and `param` files correspond to the trained model files. `param` file corresponds to a model definition and `symbol` to weights in a specific epoch.

4. How would you load a pre-trained model from a checkpoint at epoch 10?

   You would load.checkpoint function and pass model name and checkpoint number as a parameters, such as:

   2. `mx.load_checkpoint(MODEL_NAME, 10, mx.FeedForward);`

3. How can you adjust a neural network for a custom problem?

   It is by replacing the last `Softmax Output` and `FullyConnected` layers with custom definition and running `fit` on a custom dataset.

Chapter 8

1. How do you define C++ code in Julia?

   You put in between `cxx"""` and `"""` tags, such as `cxx""" <C++ CODE> """`

2. How do you call C++ functions in Julia?

   C++ functions are called using `@cxx` macro, such as `@cxx function_name();`

3. When and why you need to destroy object coming from Open CV?

   You need to destroy objects to release memory allocated by C++.

4. What type of classifier we have used to run face detection?

   We have used `Haar` cascade classifier in Open CV.

5. What is the number of classes we predict in Object detection using MobileNet-SSD
section?

   The default setup comes with 20 classes. It is possible to retrain the dataset to any number of classes.

Other Books You May Enjoy

If you enjoyed this book, you may be interested in these other books by Packt:

Julia High Performance
Avik Sengupta

ISBN: 978-1-78588-091-9

- Discover the secrets behind Julia's speed
- Get a sense of the possibilities and limitations of Julia's performance
- Analyze the performance of Julia programs
- Measure the time and memory taken by Julia programs
- Create fast machine code using Julia's type information
- Define and call functions without compromising Julia's performance
- Understand number types in Julia
- Use Julia arrays to write high performance code
- Get an overview of Julia's distributed computing capabilities

Julia for Data Science
Anshul Joshi

ISBN: 978-1-78528-969-9

- Apply statistical models in Julia for data-driven decisions
- Understanding the process of data munging and data preparation using Julia
- Explore techniques to visualize data using Julia and D3 based packages
- Using Julia to create self-learning systems using cutting edge machine learning algorithms
- Create supervised and unsupervised machine learning systems using Julia. Also, explore ensemble models
- Build a recommendation engine in Julia
- Dive into Julia's deep learning framework and build a system using Mocha.jl

Leave a review - let other readers know what you think

Please share your thoughts on this book with others by leaving a review on the site that you bought it from. If you purchased the book from Amazon, please leave us an honest review on this book's Amazon page. This is vital so that other potential readers can see and use your unbiased opinion to make purchasing decisions, we can understand what our customers think about our products, and our authors can see your feedback on the title that they have worked with Packt to create. It will only take a few minutes of your time, but is valuable to other potential customers, our authors, and Packt. Thank you!

Index

image erosion 46

www.ingramcontent.com/pod-product-compliance
Lightning Source LLC
LaVergne TN
LVHW081525050326
832903LV00025B/1633